"This radical multi-dimensional generative cubist text with the simplest words imaginable continues to alter and shape poetics into the post post modernist future. We have Gertrude Stein's 'mind grammar' operating at full tilt, with unpredictability, wit and sensory prevarication. Look to the 'minutest particulars,' Blake admonished, and here she does just that: 'it is a winning cake.' Salvos to the editor and salient 'afterword' that give belletristic notes and political perspective as well. A unique edition."

—Anne Waldman, The Jack Kerouac School
of Disembodied Poetics

TENDER BUTTONS

GERTRUDE STEIN

TENDER BUTTONS

THE CORRECTED CENTENNIAL EDITION

Edited, with a Note on the Text, by Seth Perlow

Afterword by Juliana Spahr

City Lights Books • San Francisco

Originally published in 1914 by Claire Maire

First City Lights edition, 2014

Cover art: *La Femme au Livre (Woman with Book)*, by Juan Gris, Oil on canvas,1926

Library of Congress Cataloging-in-Publication Data
Stein, Gertrude, 1874-1946.
 Tender buttons / Gertrude Stein ; edited, with a note on the text, by Seth Perlow ; afterword by Juliana Spahr. -- Corrected centennial edition.
    pages cm
 ISBN 978-0-87286-635-5
 I. Perlow, Seth. II. Title.

PS3537.T323T4 2014
818'.5209--dc23

                        2013046210

City Lights Books are published at the City Lights Bookstore,
261 Columbus Avenue, San Francisco, CA 94133.
www.citylights.com

C O N T E N T S

TENDER BUTTONS

Objects ∴ Food ∴ Rooms

OBJECTS

A CARAFE, THAT IS A BLIND GLASS.

A kind in glass and a cousin, a spectacle and nothing strange a single hurt color and an arrangement in a system to pointing. All this and not ordinary, not unordered in not resembling. The difference is spreading.

GLAZED GLITTER.

Nickel, what is nickel, it is originally rid of a cover.

The change in that is that red weakens an hour. The change has come. There is no search. But there is, there is that hope and that interpretation and sometime, surely any s is unwelcome, sometime there is breath and there will be a sinecure and charming very charming is that clean and cleansing. Certainly glittering is handsome and convincing.

There is no gratitude in mercy and in medicine. There can be breakages in Japanese. That is no programme. That is no color chosen. It was chosen yesterday, that showed spitting and perhaps washing and polishing. It certainly showed no obligation and perhaps if borrowing is not natural there is some use in giving.

A SUBSTANCE IN A CUSHION.

The change of color is likely and a difference a very little difference is prepared. Sugar is not a vegetable.

Callous is something that hardening leaves behind what will be soft if there is a genuine interest in there being present as many girls as men. Does this change. It shows that dirt is clean when there is a volume.

A cushion has that cover. Supposing you do not like to change, supposing it is very clear that there is no change in appearance, supposing that there is regularity and a costume is that any the worse than an oyster and an exchange. Come to season that is there any extreme use in feathers and cotton. Is there not much more joy in a table and more chairs and very likely roundness and a place to put them.

A circle of fine card board and a chance to see a tassel.

What is the use of a violent kind of delightfulness if there is no pleasure in not getting tired of it. The question does not come before there is a quotation. In any kind of place there is a top to covering and it is a pleasure at any rate there is some venturing in refusing to believe nonsense. It shows what use there is in a whole piece if one uses it and it is extreme and very likely the little things could be dearer but in any case there is a bargain and if there is the best thing to do is to take it away and wear it and then be reckless be reckless and resolved on returning gratitude.

Light blue and the same red with purple makes a change. It shows that there is no mistake. Any pink shows that and very likely it is reasonable. Very likely there should not be a finer fancy present. Some increase means a calamity and this is the best preparation for three and more being together. A little calm is so ordinary and in any case there is sweetness and some of that.

A seal and matches and a swan and ivy and a suit.

A closet, a closet does not connect under the bed. The band if it is white and black, the band has a green string. A sight a whole sight and a little groan grinding makes a trimming such a sweet singing trimming and a red thing not a round thing but a white thing, a red thing and a white thing.

The disgrace is not in carelessness nor even in sewing it comes out out of the way.

What is the sash like. The sash is not like anything mustard it is not like a same thing that has stripes, it is not even more hurt than that, it has a little top.

A BOX.

Out of kindness comes redness and out of rudeness comes rapid same question, out of an eye comes research, out of selection comes painful cattle. So then the order is that a white way of being round is something suggesting a pin and is it disappointing, it is not, it is so rudimentary to be analysed and see a fine substance strangely, it is so earnest to have a green point not to red but to point again.

A PIECE OF COFFEE.

More of double.

A place in no new table.

A single image is not splendor. Dirty is yellow. A sign of more in not mentioned. A piece of coffee is not a detainer. The resemblance to yellow is dirtier and distincter. The clean mixture is whiter and not coal color, never more coal color than altogether.

The sight of a reason, the same sight slighter, the sight of a simpler negative answer, the same sore sounder, the intention to wishing, the same splendor, the same furniture.

The time to show a message is when too late and later there is no hanging in a blight.

A not torn rose-wood color. If it is not dangerous then a pleasure and more than any other if it is cheap is not cheaper. The amusing side is that the sooner there are no fewer the more certain is the necessity dwindled. Supposing that the case contained rose wood and a color. Supposing that there was no reason for a distress and more likely for a number, supposing that there was no astonishment, is it not necessary to mingle astonishment.

The settling of stationing cleaning is one way not to shatter scatter and scattering. The one way to use custom is to use soap and silk for cleaning. The one way to see cotton is to have a design concentrating the illusion and the illustration. The perfect way is to accustom the thing to have a lining and the shape of a ribbon and to be solid, quite solid in standing and to use heaviness in morning. It is light enough in that. It has that shape nicely. Very nicely may not be exaggerating. Very strongly may be sincerely fainting. May be strangely flattering. May not be strange in everything. May not be strange to.

DIRT AND NOT COPPER.

Dirt and not copper makes a color darker. It makes the shape so heavy and makes no melody harder. It makes mercy and relaxation and even a strength to spread a table fuller. There are more places not empty. They see cover.

NOTHING ELEGANT.

A charm a single charm is doubtful. If the red is rose and there is a gate surrounding it, if inside is let in and there places change then certainly something is upright. It is earnest.

MILDRED'S UMBRELLA.

A cause and no curve, a cause and loud enough, a cause and extra a loud clash and an extra wagon, a sign of extra, a sac a small sac and an established color and cunning, a slender grey and no ribbon, this means a loss a great loss a restitution.

A METHOD OF A CLOAK.

A single climb to a line, a straight exchange to a cane, a desperate adventure and courage and a clock, all this which is a system, which has feeling, which has resignation and success, all makes an attractive black silver.

A RED STAMP.

If lilies are lily white if they exhaust noise and distance and even dust, if they dusty will dirt a surface that has no extreme grace, if they do this and it is not necessary it is not at all necessary if they do this they need a catalogue.

A BOX.

A large box is handily made of what is necessary to replace any substance. Suppose an example is necessary, the plainer it is made the more reason there is for some outward recognition that there is a result.

A box is made sometimes and them to see to see to it neatly and to have the holes stopped up makes it necessary to use paper.

A custom which is necessary when a box is used and taken is that a large part of the time there are three which have different connections. The one is on the table. The two are on the table. The three are on the table. The one, one is the same length as is shown by the cover being longer. The other is different there is more cover that shows it. The other is different and that makes the corners have the same shade the eight are in singular arrangement to make four necessary.

Lax, to have corners, to be lighter than some weight, to indicate a wedding journey, to last brown and not curious, to be wealthy, cigarettes are established by length and by doubling.

Left open, to be left pounded, to be left closed, to be circulating in summer and winter, and sick color that is grey that is not dusty and red shows, to be sure cigarettes do measure an empty length sooner than a choice in color.

Winged, to be winged means that white is yellow and pieces pieces that are brown are dust color if dust is washed off, then it is choice that is to say it is fitting cigarettes sooner than paper.

An increase why is an increase idle, why is silver cloister, why is the spark brighter, if it is brighter is there any result, hardly more than ever.

A PLATE.

An occasion for a plate, an occasional resource is in buying and how soon does washing enable a selection of the same thing neater. If the party is small a clever song is in order.

Plates and a dinner set of colored china. Pack together a string and enough with it to protect the center, cause a considerable haste and gather more as it is cooling, collect more trembling and not any even trembling, cause a whole thing to be a church.

A sad size a size that is not sad is blue as every bit of blue is precocious. A kind of green a game in green and nothing flat nothing quite flat and more round, nothing a particular color strangely, nothing breaking the losing of no little piece.

A splendid address a really splendid address is not shown by giving a flower freely, it is not shown by a mark or by wetting.

Cut cut in white, cut in white so lately. Cut more than any other and show it. Show it in the stem and in starting and in evening coming complication.

A lamp is not the only sign of glass. The lamp and the cake are not the only sign of stone. The lamp and the cake and the cover are not the only necessity altogether.

A plan a hearty plan, a compressed disease and no coffee, not even a card or a change to incline each way, a plan that has that excess and that break is the one that shows filling.

A SELTZER BOTTLE.

Any neglect of many particles to a cracking, any neglect of this makes around it what is lead in color and certainly discolor in silver. The use of this is manifold. Supposing a certain time selected is assured, suppose it is even necessary, suppose no other extract is permitted and no more handling is needed, suppose the rest of the message is mixed with a very long slender needle and even if it could be any black border, supposing all this altogether made a dress and suppose it was actual, suppose the mean way to state it was occasional, if you suppose this in August and even more melodiously, if you suppose this even in the necessary incident of there certainly being no middle in summer and winter, suppose this and an elegant settlement a very elegant settlement is more than of consequence, it is not final and sufficient and substituted. This which was so kindly a present was constant.

A LONG DRESS.

What is the current that makes machinery, that makes it crackle, what is the current that presents a long line and a necessary waist. What is this current.

What is the wind, what is it.

Where is the serene length, it is there and a dark place is not a dark place, only a white and red are black, only a yellow and green are blue, a pink is scarlet, a bow is every color. A line distinguishes it. A line just distinguishes it.

A RED HAT.

A dark grey, a very dark grey, a quite dark grey is monstrous ordinarily, it is so monstrous because there is no red in it. If red is in everything it is not necessary. Is that not an argument for any use of it and even so is there any place that is better, is there any place that has so much stretched out.

A BLUE COAT.

A blue coat is guided guided away, guided and guided away, that is the particular color that is used for that length and not any width not even more than a shadow.

A PIANO.

If the speed is open, if the color is careless, if the event is overtaken, if the selection of a strong scent is not awkward, if the button holder is held by all the waving color and there is no color, not any color. If there is no dirt in a pin and there can be none scarcely, if there is not then the place is the same as up standing.

This is no dark custom and it even is not acted in any such a way that a restraint is not spread. That is spread, it shuts and it lifts and awkwardly not awkwardly the center is in standing.

A CHAIR.

A widow in a wise veil and more garments shows that shadows are even. It addresses no more, it shadows the stage and learning. A regular arrangement, the severest and the most preserved is that which has the arrangement not more than always authorised.

A suitable establishment, well housed, practical, patient and staring, a suitable bedding, very suitable and not more particularly than complaining, anything suitable is so necessary.

A fact is that when the direction is just like that, no more, longer, sudden and at the same time not any sofa, the main action is that without a blaming there is no custody.

Practice measurement, practice the sign that means that really means a necessary betrayal, in showing that there is wearing.

Hope, what is a spectacle, a spectacle is the resemblance between the circular side place and nothing else, nothing else.

To choose it is ended, it is actual and more than that it has it certainly has the same treat, and a seat all that is practiced and more easily much more easily ordinarily.

Pick a barn, a whole barn, and bend more slender accents than have ever been necessary, shine in the darkness necessarily.

Actually not aching, actually not aching, a stubborn bloom is so artificial and even more than that, it is a spectacle, it is a binding accident, it is animosity and accentuation.

If the chance to dirty diminishing is necessary, if it is why is there no complexion, why is there no rubbing, why is there no special protection.

A FRIGHTFUL RELEASE.

A bag which was left and not only taken but turned away was not found. The place was shown to be very like the last time. A piece was not exchanged, not a bit of it, a piece was left over. The rest was mismanaged.

A PURSE.

A purse was not green, it was not straw color, it was hardly seen and it had a use a long use and the chain, the chain was never missing, it was not misplaced, it showed that it was open, that is all that it showed.

A MOUNTED UMBRELLA.

What was the use of not leaving it there where it would hang what was the use if there was no chance of ever seeing it come there and show that it was handsome and right in the way it showed it. The lesson is to learn that it does show it, that it shows it and that nothing, that there is nothing, that there is no more to do about it and just so much more is there plenty of reason for making an exchange.

A CLOTH.

Enough cloth is plenty and more, more is almost enough for that and besides if there is no more spreading is there plenty of room for it. Any occasion shows the best way.

More.

An elegant use of foliage and grace and a little piece of white cloth and oil.

Wondering so winningly in several kinds of oceans is the reason that makes red so regular and enthusiastic. The reason that there is more snips are the same shining very colored rid of no round color.

A new cup and saucer.

Enthusiastically hurting a clouded yellow bud and saucer, enthusiastically so is the bite in the ribbon.

Objects.

Within, within the cut and slender joint alone, with sudden equals and no more than three, two in the center make two one side.

If the elbow is long and it is filled so then the best example is all together.

The kind of show is made by squeezing.

Eye glasses.

A color in shaving, a saloon is well placed in the center of an alley.

A CUTLET.

A blind agitation is manly and uttermost.

CARELESS WATER.

No cup is broken in more places and mended, that is to say a plate is broken and mending does do that it shows that culture is Japanese. It shows the whole element of angels and orders. It does more to choosing and it does more to that ministering counting. It does, it does change in more water.

Supposing a single piece is a hair supposing more of them are orderly, does that show that strength, does that show that joint, does that show that balloon famously. Does it.

A PAPER.

A courteous occasion makes a paper show no such occasion and this makes readiness and eyesight and likeness and a stool.

A DRAWING.

The meaning of this is entirely and best to say the mark, best to say it best to show sudden places, best to make bitter, best to make the length tall and nothing broader, anything between the half.

Water raining.

Water astonishing and difficult altogether makes a meadow and a stroke.

Cold climate.

A season in yellow sold extra strings makes lying places.

Malachite.

The sudden spoon is the same in no size. The sudden spoon is the wound in the decision.

An umbrella.

Coloring high means that the strange reason is in front not more in front behind. Not more in front in peace of the dot.

A petticoat.

A light white, a disgrace, an ink spot, a rosy charm.

A waist.

A star glide, a single frantic sullenness, a single financial grass greediness.

Object that is in wood. Hold the pine, hold the dark, hold in the rush, make the bottom.

A piece of crystal. A change, in a change that is remarkable there is no reason to say that there was a time.

A wooden object gilded. A country climb is the best disgrace, a couple of practices any of them in order is so left.

A TIME TO EAT.

A pleasant simple habitual and tyrannical and authorised and educated and resumed and articulate separation. This is not tardy.

A LITTLE BIT OF A TUMBLER.

A shining indication of yellow consists in there having been more of the same color than could have been expected when all four were bought. This was the hope which made the six and seven have no use for any more places and this necessarily spread into nothing. Spread into nothing.

A FIRE.

What was the use of a whole time to send and not send if there was to be the kind of thing that made that come in. A letter was nicely sent.

A HANDKERCHIEF.

A winning of all the blessings, a sample not a sample because there is no worry.

Red roses.

A cool red rose and a pink cut pink, a collapse and a sold hole, a little less hot.

In between.

In between a place and candy is a narrow foot path that shows more mounting than anything, so much really that a calling meaning a bolster measured a whole thing with that. A virgin a whole virgin is judged made and so between curves and outlines and real seasons and more out glasses and a perfectly unprecedented arrangement between old ladies and mild colds there is no satin wood shining.

Colored Hats.

Colored hats are necessary to show that curls are worn by an addition of blank spaces, this makes the difference between single lines and broad stomachs, the least thing is lightening, the least thing means a little flower and a big delay a big delay that makes more nurses than little women really little women. So clean is a light that nearly all of it shows pearls and little ways. A large hat is tall and me and all custard whole.

A FEATHER.

A feather is trimmed, it is trimmed by the light and the bug and the post, it is trimmed by little leaning and by all sorts of mounted reserves and loud volumes. It is surely cohesive.

A BROWN.

A brown which is not liquid not more so is relaxed and yet there is a change, a news is pressing.

A LITTLE CALLED PAULINE.

A little called anything shows shudders.

Come and say what prints all day. A whole few watermelon. There is no pope.

No cut in pennies and little dressing and choose wide soles and little spats really little spices.

A little lace makes boils. This is not true.

Gracious of gracious and a stamp a blue green white bow a blue green lean, lean on the top.

If it is absurd then it is leadish and nearly set in where there is a tight head.

A peaceful life to arise her, moon and moon and moon. A letter a cold sleeve a blanket a shaving house and nearly the best and regular window.

Nearer in fairy sea, nearer and farther, show white has lime in sight, show a stitch of ten. Count, count more so that thicker and thicker is leaning.

I hope she has her cow. Bidding a wedding, widening received treading, little leading, mention nothing.

Cough out cough out in the leather and really feather it is not for.

Please could, please could, jam it not plus more sit in when.

A SOUND.

Elephant beaten with candy and little pops and chews all bolts and reckless reckless rats, this is this.

A TABLE.

A table means does it not my dear it means a whole steadiness. Is it likely that a change.

A table means more than a glass even a looking glass is tall. A table means necessary places and a revision a revision of a little thing it means it does mean that there has been a stand, a stand where it did shake.

SHOES.

To be a wall with a damper a stream of pounding way and nearly enough choice makes a steady midnight. It is pus.

A shallow hole rose on red, a shallow hole in and in this makes ale less. It shows shine.

A DOG.

A little monkey goes like a donkey that means to say that means to say that more sighs last goes. Leave with it. A little monkey goes like a donkey.

A WHITE HUNTER.

A white hunter is nearly crazy.

A LEAVE.

In the middle of a tiny spot and nearly bare there is a nice thing to say that wrist is leading. Wrist is leading.

SUPPOSE AN EYES.

Suppose it is within a gate which open is open at the hour of closing summer that is to say it is so.

All the seats are needing blackening. A white dress is in sign. A soldier a real soldier has a worn lace a worn lace of different sizes that is to say if he can read, if he can read he is a size to show shutting up twenty-four.

Go red go red, laugh white.

Suppose a collapse in rubbed purr, in rubbed purr get.

Little sales ladies little sales ladies little saddles of mutton.

Little sales of leather and such beautiful beautiful, beautiful beautiful.

A SHAWL.

A shawl is a hat and hurt and a red balloon and an under coat and a sizer a sizer of talk.

A shawl is a wedding, a piece of wax a little build. A shawl.

Pick a ticket, pick it in strange steps and with hollows. There is hollow hollow belt, a belt is a shawl.

A plate that has a little bobble, all of them, any so.

Please a round it is ticket.

It was a mistake to state that a laugh and a lip and a laid climb and a depot and a cultivator and little choosing is a point it.

BOOK.

Book was there, it was there. Book was there. Stop it, stop it, it was a cleaner, a wet cleaner and it was not where it was wet, it was not high, it was directly placed back, not back again, back, it was returned, it was needless, it put a bank, a bank when, a bank care.

Suppose a man a realistic expression of resolute reliability suggests pleasing itself white all white and no head does that mean soap. It does not so. It means kind wavers and little chance to beside beside rest. A plain.

Suppose ear rings, that is one way to breed, breed that. Oh chance to say, oh nice old pole. Next best and nearest a pillar. Chest not valuable, be papered.

Cover up cover up the two with a little piece of string and hope rose and green, green.

Please a plate, put a match to the seam and really then really then, really then it is a remark that joins many many lead games. It is a sister and sister and a flower and a flower and a dog and a colored sky a sky colored grey and nearly that nearly that let.

Peeled pencil, choke.

Rub her coke.

It was black, black took.

Black ink best wheel bale brown.

Excel lent not a hull house, not a pea soup, no bill no care, no precise no past pearl pearl goat.

This is this dress, aider.

Aider, why, aider why whow, whow stop touch, aider whow, aider stop the muncher, muncher munchers.

A jack in kill her, a jack in, makes a meadowed king, makes a to let.

F O O D

ROASTBEEF   MUTTON   BREAKFAST   SUGAR
CRANBERRIES   MILK   EGGS   APPLE   TAILS
LUNCH   CUPS   RHUBARB   SINGLE FISH   CAKE   CUSTARD
POTATOES   ASPARAGUS   BUTTER   END OF SUMMER
SAUSAGES   CELERY   VEAL   VEGETABLE   COOKING
CHICKEN   PASTRY   CREAM   CUCUMBER   DINNER
DINING   EATING   SALAD   SAUCE   SALMON   ORANGE
COCOA AND CLEAR SOUP AND ORANGES AND OAT-MEAL
SALAD DRESSING AND AN ARTICHOKE   A CENTER IN A TABLE.

ROASTBEEF.

In the inside there is sleeping, in the outside there is reddening, in the morning there is meaning, in the evening there is feeling. In the evening there is feeling. In feeling anything is resting, in feeling anything is mounting, in feeling there is resignation, in feeling there is recognition, in feeling there is recurrence and entirely mistaken there is pinching. All the standards have steamers and all the curtains have bed linen and all the yellow has discrimination and all the circle has circling. This makes sand.

Very well. Certainly the length is thinner and the rest, the round rest has a longer summer. To shine, why not shine, to shine, to station, to enlarge, to hurry the measure all this means nothing if there is singing, if there is singing then there is the resumption.

The change the dirt, not to change dirt means that there is no beefsteak and not to have that is no obstruction, it is so easy to exchange meaning, it is so easy to see the difference. The difference is that a plain resource is not entangled with thickness and it does not mean that thickness shows such cutting, it does mean that a meadow is useful and a cow absurd. It does not mean that there are tears, it does not mean that exudation is cumbersome, it means no more than a memory, a choice and a reestablishment, it means more than any escape from a surrounding extra. All the time that there is use there is use and any time there is a surface there is a surface, and every time there is an exception there is an exception and every time there is a division there is a dividing. Any time there is a surface there is a surface and every time there is a suggestion there is a suggestion and every time there is silence there is silence and every time that is languid there is that there then and not oftener, not always, not particular, tender and changing and external and central and surrounded and singular and simple and the same and the surface and the circle and the shine and the succor and the white and the same and the better and the red and the same and the center and the yellow and the tender and the better, and altogether.

Considering the circumstances there is no occasion for a reduction, considering that there is no pealing there is no occasion for an obligation, considering that there is no outrage there is no necessity for any reparation, considering that there is no particle sodden there is no occasion for deliberation. Considering everything and which way the turn is tending, considering everything why is there no restraint, considering everything what makes the place settle and the plate distinguish some specialties. The whole thing is not understood and this is not strange considering that there is no education, this is not strange because having that certainly does show the difference in cutting, it shows that when there is turning there is no distress.

In kind, in a control, in a period, in the alteration of pigeons, in kind cuts and thick and thin spaces, in kind ham and different colors, the length of leaning a strong thing outside not to make a sound but to suggest a crust, the principal taste is when there is a whole chance to be reasonable, this does not mean that there is overtaking, this means nothing precious, this means clearly that the chance to exercise is a social success. So then the sound is not obtrusive. Suppose it is obtrusive, suppose it is. What is certainly the desertion is not a reduced description, a description is not a birthday.

Lovely snipe and tender turn, excellent vapor and slender butter, all the splinter and the trunk, all the poisonous darkning drunk, all the joy in weak success, all the joyful tenderness, all the section and the tea, all the stouter symmetry.

Around the size that is small, inside the stern that is the middle, besides the remains that are praying, inside the between that is turning, all the region is measuring and melting is exaggerating.

Rectangular ribbon does not mean that there is no eruption it means that if there is no place to hold there is no place to spread. Kindness is not earnest, it is not assiduous it is not revered.

Room to comb chickens and feathers and ripe purple, room to curve single plates and large sets and second silver, room to send everything away, room to save heat and distemper, room to search a light that is simpler, all room has no shadow.

There is no use there is no use at all in smell, in taste, in teeth, in toast, in anything, there is no use at all and the respect is mutual.

Why should that which is uneven, that which is resumed, that which is tolerable why should all this resemble a smell, a thing is there, it whistles, it is not narrower, why is there no obligation to stay away and yet courage, courage is everywhere and the best remains to stay.

If there could be that which is contained in that which is felt there would be a chair where there are chairs and there would be no more denial about a clatter. A clatter is not a smell. All this is good.

The Saturday evening which is Sunday is every week day. What choice is there when there is a difference. A regulation is not active. Thirstiness is not equal division.

Anyway, to be older and ageder is not a surfeit nor a suction, it is not dated and careful, it is not dirty. Any little thing is clean, rubbing is black. Why should ancient lambs be goats and young colts and never beef, why should they, they should because there is so much difference in age.

A sound, a whole sound is not separation, a whole sound is in an order.

Suppose there is a pigeon, suppose there is.

Looseness, why is there a shadow in a kitchen, there is a shadow in a kitchen because every little thing is bigger.

The time when there are four choices and there are four choices in a difference, the time when there are four choices there is a kind and there is a kind. There is a kind. There is a kind. Supposing there is a bone, there is a bone. Supposing there are bones. There are bones. When there are bones there is no supposing there are bones. There are bones and there is that consuming. The kindly way to feel separating is to have a space between. This shows a likeness.

Hope in gates, hope in spoons, hope in doors, hope in tables, no hope in daintiness and determination. Hope in dates.

Tin is not a can and a stove is hardly. Tin is not necessary and neither is a stretcher. Tin is never narrow and thick.

Color is in coal. Coal is outlasting roasting and a spoonful, a whole spoon that is full is not spilling. Coal any coal is copper.

Claiming nothing, not claiming anything, not a claim in everything, collecting claiming, all this makes a harmony, it even makes a succession.

Sincerely gracious one morning, sincerely graciously trembling, sincere in gracious eloping, all this makes a furnace and a blanket. All this shows quantity.

Like an eye, not so much more, not any searching, no compliments.

Please be the beef, please beef, pleasure is not wailing. Please beef, please be carved clear, please be a case of consideration.

Search a neglect. A sale, any greatness is a stall and there is no memory, there is no clear collection.

A satin sight, what is a trick, no trick is mountainous and the color, all the rush is in the blood.

Bargaining for a little, bargain for a touch, a liberty, an estrangement, a characteristic turkey.

Please spice, please no name, place a whole weight, sink into a standard rising, raise a circle, choose a right around, make the resonance accounted and gather green any collar.

To bury a slender chicken, to raise an old feather, to surround a garland and to bake a pole splinter, to suggest a repose and to settle simply, to surrender one another, to succeed saving simpler, to satisfy a singularity and not to be blinder, to sugar nothing darker and to read redder, to have the color better, to sort out dinner, to remain together, to surprise no sinner, to curve nothing sweeter, to continue thinner, to increase in resting recreation to design string not dimmer.

Cloudiness what is cloudiness, is it a lining, is it a roll, is it melting.

The sooner there is jerking, the sooner freshness is tender, the sooner the round it is not round the sooner it is withdrawn in cutting, the sooner the measure means service, the sooner there is chinking, the sooner there is sadder than salad, the sooner there is none do her, the sooner there is no choice, the sooner there is a gloom freer, the same sooner and more sooner, this is no error in hurry and in pressure and in opposition to consideration.

A recital, what is a recital, it is an organ and use does not strengthen valor, it soothes medicine.

A transfer, a large transfer, a little transfer, some transfer, clouds and tracks do transfer, a transfer is not neglected.

Pride, when is there perfect pretence, there is no more than yesterday and ordinary.

A sentence of a vagueness that is violence is authority and a mission and stumbling and also certainly also a prison. Calmness, calm is beside the plate and in way in. There is no turn in terror. There is no volume in sound.

There is coagulation in cold and there is none in prudence. Something is preserved and the evening is long and the colder spring has sudden shadows in a sun. All the stain is tender and lilacs really lilacs are disturbed. Why is the perfect reestablishment practiced and prized, why is it composed. The result the pure result is juice and size and baking and exhibition and nonchalance and sacrifice and volume and a section in division and the surrounding recognition and horticulture and no murmur. This is a result. There is no superposition and circumstance, there is hardness and a reason and the rest and remainder. There is no delight and no mathematics.

MUTTON.

A letter which can wither, a learning which can suffer and an outrage which is simultaneous is principal.

Student, students are merciful and recognised they chew something.

Hate rests that is solid and sparse and all in a shape and largely very largely. Interleaved and successive and a sample of smell all this makes a certainty a shade.

Light curls very light curls have no more curliness than soup. This is not a subject.

Change a single stream of denting and change it hurriedly, what does it express, it expresses nausea. Like a very strange likeness and pink, like that and not more like that than the same resemblance and not more like that than no middle space in cutting.

An eye glass, what is an eye glass, it is water. A splendid specimen, what is it when it is little and tender so that there are parts. A center can place and four are no more and two and two are not middle.

Melting and not minding, safety and powder, a particular recollection and a sincere solitude all this makes shunning so thorough and so unrepeated and surely if there is anything left it is a bone. It is not solitary.

Any space is not quiet it is so likely to be shiny. Darkness very dark darkness is sectional. There is a way to see in onion and surely very surely rhubarb and a tomatoe, surely very surely there is that seeding. A little thing in is a little thing.

Mud and water were not present and not any more of either. Silk and stockings were not present and not any more of either. A receptacle and a symbol and no monster were present and no more. This made a piece show and was it a kindness, it can be asked was it a kindness to have it warmer, was it a kindness and does gliding mean more. Does it.

Does it dirty a ceiling. It does not. Is it dainty, it is if prices are sweet. Is it lamentable, it is not if there is no undertaker. Is it curious, it is not when there is youth. All this makes a line, it even makes no more. All this makes cherries. The reason that there is a suggestion in variety is due to this that there is a burst of mixed music.

A temptation any temptation is an exclamation if there are misdeeds and little bones. It is not astonishing that bones mingle as they vary not at all and in any case why is a bone outstanding, it is so because the circumstance that does not make a cake and character is so easily churned and cherished.

Mouse and mountain and a quiver, a quaint statue and pain in an exterior and silence more silence louder shows salmon a mischief intender. A cake, a real salve made of mutton and liquor, a specially retained rinsing and an established cork and blazing, this which resignation influences and restrains, restrains more altogether. A sign is the specimen spoken.

A meal in mutton, mutton, why is lamb cheaper, it is cheaper because so little is more. Lecture, lecture and repeat instruction.

BREAKFAST.

A change, a final change includes potatoes. This is no authority for the abuse of cheese. What language can instruct any fellow.

A shining breakfast, a breakfast shining, no dispute, no practice, nothing, nothing at all.

A sudden slice changes the whole plate, it does so suddenly.

An imitation, more imitation, imitations succeed imitations.

Anything that is decent, anything that is present, a calm and a cook and more singularly still a shelter, all these show the need of clamor. What is the custom, the custom is in the center.

What is a loving tongue and pepper and more fish than there is when tears many tears are necessary. The tongue and the salmon, there is not salmon when brown is a color, there is salmon when there is no meaning to an early morning being pleasanter. There is no salmon, there are no tea cups, there are the same kind of mushes as are used as stomachers by the eating hopes that makes eggs delicious. Drink is likely to stir a certain respect for an egg cup and more water melon than was ever eaten yesterday. Beer is neglected and cocoanut is famous. Coffee all coffee and a sample of soup all soup these are the choice of a baker. A white cup means a wedding. A wet cup means a vacation. A strong cup means an especial regulation. A single cup means a capital arrangement between the drawer and the place that is open.

Price a price is not in language, it is not in custom, it is not in praise.

A colored loss, why is there no leisure. If the persecution is so outrageous that nothing is solemn is there any occasion for persuasion.

A grey turn to a top and bottom, a silent pocketful of much heating, all the pliable succession of surrendering makes an ingenious joy.

A breeze in a jar and even then silence, a special anticipation in a rack, a gurgle a whole gurgle and more cheese than almost anything, is this an astonishment, does this incline more than the original division between a tray and a talking arrangement and even then a calling into another room gently with some chicken in any way.

A bent way that is a way to declare that the best is all

together, a bent way shows no result, it shows a slight restraint, it shows a necessity for retraction.

Suspect a single buttered flower, suspect it certainly, suspect it and then glide, does that not alter a counting.

A hurt mended stick, a hurt mended cup, a hurt mended article of exceptional relaxation and annoyance, a hurt mended, hurt and mended is so necessary that no mistake is intended.

What is more likely than a roast, nothing really and yet it is never disappointed singularly.

A steady cake, any steady cake is perfect and not plain, any steady cake has a mounting reason and more than that it has singular crusts. A season of more is a season that is instead. A season of many is not more a season than most.

Take no remedy lightly, take no urging intently, take no separation leniently, beware of no lake and no larder.

Burden the cracked wet soaking sack heavily, burden it so that it is an institution in fright and in climate and in the best plan that there can be.

An ordinary color, a color is that strange mixture which makes, which does make which does not make a ripe juice, which does not make a mat.

A work which is a winding a real winding of the cloaking of a relaxing rescue. This which is so cool is not dusting, it is not dirtying in smelling, it could use white water, it could use more extraordinarily and in no solitude altogether. This which is so not winsome and not widened and really not so dipped as dainty and really dainty, very dainty, ordinarily, dainty, a dainty, not in that dainty and dainty. If the time is determined, if it is determined and there is reunion there is reunion with that then outline, then there is in that a piercing shutter, all of a piercing shouter, all of a quite weather, all of a withered exterior, all of that in most violent likely.

An excuse is not dreariness, a single plate is not butter, a single weight is not excitement, a solitary crumbling is not only martial.

A mixed protection, very mixed with the same actual intentional unstrangeness and riding, a single action caused necessarily is not more a sign than a minister.

Seat a knife near a cage and very near a decision and more nearly a timely working cat and scissors. Do this temporarily and make no more mistake in standing. Spread it all and arrange the white place, does this show in the house, does it not show in the green that is not necessary for that color, does it not even show in the explanation and singularly not at all stationary.

SUGAR.

A violent luck and a whole sample and even then quiet.

Water is squeezing, water is almost squeezing on lard. Water, water is a mountain and it is selected and it is so practical that there is no use in money. A mind under is exact and so it is necessary to have a mouth and eye glasses.

A question of sudden rises and more time than awfulness is so easy and shady. There is precisely that noise.

A peck a small piece not privately overseen, not at all not a slice, not at all crestfallen and open, not at all mounting and chaining and evenly surpassing, all the bidding comes to tea.

A separation is not tightly in worsted and sauce, it is so kept well and sectionally.

Put it in the stew, put it to shame. A little slight shadow and a solid fine furnace.

The teasing is tender and trying and thoughtful.

The line which sets sprinkling to be a remedy is beside the best cold.

A puzzle, a monster puzzle, a heavy choking, a neglected Tuesday.

Wet crossing and a likeness, any likeness, a likeness has blisters, it has that and teeth, it has the staggering blindly and a little green, any little green is ordinary.

One, two and one, two, nine, second and five and that.

A blaze, a search in between, a cow, only any wet place, only this tune.

Cut a gas jet uglier and then pierce pierce in between the next and negligence. Choose the rate to pay and pet pet very much. A collection of all around, a signal poison, a lack of languor and more hurts at ease.

A white bird, a colored mine, a mixed orange, a dog.

Cuddling comes in continuing a change.

A piece of separate outstanding rushing is so blind with open delicacy.

A canoe is orderly. A period is solemn. A cow is accepted.

A nice old chain is widening, it is absent, it is laid by.

CRANBERRIES.

Could there not be a sudden date, could there not be in the present settlement of old age pensions, could there not be by a witness, could there be.

Count the chain, cut the grass, silence the noon and

murder flies. See the basting, undip the chart, see the way the kinds are best seen from the rest, from that and untidy.

Cut the whole space into twenty four spaces and then and then is there a yellow color, there is but it is smelled, it is then put where it is and nothing stolen.

A remarkable degree of red means that, a remarkable exchange is made.

Climbing all together in when there is a solid chance of soiling no more than a dirty thing, coloring all of it in steadying is jelly.

Just as it is suffering, just as it is succeeded, just as it is moist so is there no countering.

MILK.

A white egg and a colored pan and a cabbage showing settlement, a constant increase.

A cold in a nose, a single cold nose makes an excuse. Two are more necessary.

All the goods are stolen, all the blisters are in the cup.

Cooking, cooking is the recognition between sudden and nearly sudden very little and all large holes.

A real pint, one that is open and closed and in the middle is so bad.

Tender colds, seen eye holders, all work, the best of change, the meaning, the dark red, all this and bitten, really bitten.

Guessing again and golfing again and the best men, the very best men.

MILK.

Climb up in sight climb in the whole utter needles and a guess a whole guess is hanging. Hanging hanging.

EGGS.

Kind height, kind in the right stomach with a little sudden mill.

Cunning shawl, cunning shawl to be steady.

In white in white handkerchiefs with little dots in a white belt all shadows are singular they are singular and procured and relieved.

No that is not the cows shame and a precocious sound, it is a bite.

Cut up alone the paved way which is harm. Harm is old boat and a likely dash.

APPLE.

Apple plum, carpet steak, seed clam, colored wine, calm seen, cold cream, best shake, potatoe, potatoe and no no gold work with pet, a green seen is called bake and change sweet is bready, a little piece a little piece please.

A little piece please. Cane again to the presupposed and ready eucalyptus tree, count out sherry and ripe plates and little corners of a kind of ham. This is use.

Tails.

Cold pails, cold with joy no joy.

A tiny seat that means meadows and a lapse of cuddles with cheese and nearly bats, all this went messed. The post placed a loud loose sprain. A rest is no better. It is better yet. All the time.

Lunch.

Luck in loose plaster makes holy gauge and nearly that, nearly more states, more states come in town light kite, blight not white.

A little lunch is a break in skate a little lunch so slimy, a west end of a board line is that which shows a little beneath so that necessity is a silk under wear. That is best wet. It is so natural and why is there flake, there is flake to explain exhaust.

A real cold hen is nervous is nervous with a towel with a spool with real beads. It is mostly an extra sole nearly all that shaved, shaved with an old mountain, more than that bees, more than that dinner and a bunch of likes that is to say the hearts of onions aim less.

Cold coffee with a corn a corn yellow and green mass is a gem.

Cups.

A single example of excellence is in the meat. A bent stick is surging and might all might is mental. A grand clothes is searching out a candle not that wheatly not that by more than an owl and a path. A ham is proud of cocoanut.

A cup is neglected by being all in size. It is a handle and meadows and sugar any sugar.

A cup is neglected by being full of size. It shows no shade, in come little wood cuts and blessing and nearly not that not with a wild bought in, not at all so polite, not nearly so behind.

Cups crane in. They need a pet oyster, they need it so hoary and nearly choice. The best slam is utter. Nearly be freeze.

Why is a cup a stir and a behave. Why is it so seen.

A cup is readily shaded, it has in between no sense that is to say music, memory, musical memory.

Pea nuts blame, a half sand is holey and nearly.

Rhubarb.

Rhubarb is susan not susan not seat in bunch toys not wild and laughable not in little places not in neglect and vegetable not in fold coal age not please.

Single fish.

Single fish single fish single fish egg plant single fish sight.

A sweet win and not less noisy than saddle and more ploughing and nearly well painted by little things so.

Please shade it a play. It is necessary and beside the large sort is puff.

Every way oakly, please prune it near. It is so found.

It is not the same.

CAKE.

Cake cast in went to be and needles wine needles are such.

This is to-day. A can experiment is that which makes a town, makes a town dirty, it is little please. We came back. Two bore, bore what, a mussed ash, ash when there is tin. This meant cake. It was a sign.

Another time there was extra a hat pin sought long and this dark made a display. The result was yellow. A caution, not a caution to be.

It is no use to cause a foolish number. A blanket stretch a cloud, a shame, all that bakery can tease, all that is beginning and yesterday yesterday we had it met. It means some change. No some day.

A little leaf upon a scene an ocean any where there, a bland and likely in the stream a recollection green land. Why white.

CUSTARD.

Custard is this. It has aches, aches when. Not to be. Not to be narrowly. This makes a whole little hill.

It is better than a little thing that has mellow real mellow. It is better than lakes whole lakes, it is better than seeding.

POTATOES.

Real potatoes cut in between.

POTATOES.

In the preparation of cheese, in the preparation of crackers, in the preparation of butter, in it.

ROAST POTATOES.

Roast potatoes for.

ASPARAGUS.

Asparagus in a lean in a lean to hot. This makes it art and it is wet wet weather wet weather wet.

BUTTER.

Boom in boom in, butter. Leave a grain and show it, show it. I spy.

It is a need it is a need that a flower a state flower. It is a need that a state rubber. It is a need that a state rubber is sweet and sight and a swelled stretch. It is a need. It is a need that state rubber.

Wood a supply. Clean little keep and a strange, estrange on it.

Make a little white, no and not with pit, pit on in within.

END OF SUMMER.

Little eyelets that have hammer and a check with stripes between, a lounge, in wit, in a rested development.

Sausages.

Sausages in between a glass.

There is read butter. A loaf of it is managed. Wake a question. Eat an instant, answer.

A reason for bed is this, that a decline, any decline is poison, poison is a toe a toe extractor, this means a solemn change. Hanging.

No evil is wide, any extra in leaf is so strange and singular a red breast.

Celery.

Celery tastes tastes where in curled lashes and little bits and mostly in remains.

A green acre is so selfish and so pure and so enlivened.

Veal.

Very well very well, washing is old, washing is washing.

Cold soup, cold soup clear and particular and a principal a principal question to put into.

Vegetable.

What is cut. What is cut by it. What is cut by it in.

It was a cress a crescent a cross and an unequal scream, it was upslanting, it was radiant and reasonable with little ins and red.

News. News capable of glees, cut in shoes, belike under pump of wide chalk, all this combing.

WAY LAY VEGETABLE.

Leaves in grass and mow potatoes, have a skin, hurry you up flutter.

Suppose it is ex a cake suppose it is new mercy and leave charlotte and nervous bed rows. Suppose it is meal. Suppose it is sam.

COOKING.

Alas, alas the pull alas the bell alas the coach in china, alas the little put in leaf alas the wedding butter meat, alas the receptacle, alas the back shape of mussle, mussle and soda.

CHICKEN.

Pheasant and chicken, chicken is a peculiar third.

CHICKEN.

Alas a dirty word, alas a dirty third alas a dirty third, alas a dirty bird.

CHICKEN.

Alas a doubt in case of more go to say what it is cress. What is it. Mean. Potatoe. Loaves.

CHICKEN.

Stick stick call then, stick stick sticking, sticking with a chicken. Sticking in a extra succession, sticking in.

CHAIN-BOATS.

Chain-boats are merry, are merry blew, blew west, carpet.

PASTRY.

Cutting shade, cool spades and little last beds, make violet, violet when.

CREAM.

In a plank, in a play sole, in a heated red left tree there is shut in specs with salt be where. This makes an eddy. Necessary.

CREAM.

Cream cut. Any where crumb. Left hop chambers.

CUCUMBER.

Not a razor less, not a razor, ridiculous pudding, red and relet put in, rest in a slender go in selecting, rest in, rest in in white widening.

Dinner.

Not a little fit, not a little fit sun in sat in shed more mentally.

Let us why, let us why weight, let us why winter chess, let us why way.

Only a moon to soup her, only that in the sell never be the cocups nice be, shatter it they lay.

Egg ear nuts, look a bout. Shoulder. Let it strange, sold in bell next herds.

It was a time when in the acres in late there was a wheel that shot a burst of land and needless are niggers and a sample sample set of old eaten butterflies with spoons, all of it to be are fled and measures make it, make it, yes all the one in that we see where shall not it set with a left and more so, yes there add when the longer not it shall the best in the way when all be with when shall not for there with see and chest how for another excellent and excellent and easy easy excellent and easy express e c, all to be nice all to be no so. All to be no so no so. All to be not a white old chat churner. Not to be any example of an edible apple in.

Dining.

Dining is west.

Eating.

Eat ting, eating a grand old man said roof and never never re soluble burst, not a near ring not a bewildered neck, not really any such bay.

Is it so a noise to be is it a least remain to rest, is it a so old say to be, is it a leading are been. Is it so, is it so, is it so, is it so is it so is it so.

Eel us eel us with no no pea no pea cool, no pea cool cooler, no pea cooler with a land a land cost in, with a land cost in stretches.

Eating he heat eating he heat it eating, he heat it heat eating. He heat eating.

A little piece of pay of pay owls owls such as pie, bolsters.

Will leap beat, willie well all. The rest rest oxen occasion occasion to be so purred, so purred how.

It was a ham it was a square come well it was a square remain, a square remain not it a bundle, not it a bundle so is a grip, a grip to shed bay leave bay leave draught, bay leave draw cider in low, cider in low and george. George is a mass.

EATING.

It was a shame it was a shame to stare to stare and double and relieve relieve be cut up show as by the elevation of it and out out more in the steady where the come and on and the all the shed and that.

It was a garden and belows belows straight. It was a pea, a pea pour it in its not a succession, not it a simple, not it a so election, election with.

SALAD.

It is a winning cake.

Sauce.

What is bay labored what is all be section, what is no much. Sauce sam in.

Salmon.

It was a peculiar bin a bin fond in beside.

Orange.

Why is a feel oyster an egg stir. Why is it orange center.
A show at tick and loosen loosen it so to speak sat.
It was an extra leaker with a see spoon, it was an extra licker with a see spoon.

Orange.

A type oh oh new new not no not knealer knealer of old show beefsteak, neither neither.

Oranges.

Build is all right.

Orange in.

Go lack go lack use to her.

Cocoa and clear soup and oranges and oat-meal.

Whist bottom whist close, whist clothes, woodling.

Cocoa and clear soup and oranges and oat-meal.

Pain soup, suppose it is question, suppose it is butter, real is, real is only, only excreate, only excreate a no since.

A no, a no since, a no since when, a no since when since, a no since when since a no since when since, a no since, a no since when since, a no since, a no, a no since a no since, a no since, a no since.

Salad dressing and an artichoke.

Please pale hot, please cover rose, please acre in the red stranger, please butter all the beef-steak with regular feel faces.

Salad dressing and an artichoke.

It was please it was please carriage cup in an ice-cream, in an ice-cream it was too bended bended with scissors and all this time. A whole is inside a part, a part does go away, a hole is red leaf. No choice was where there was and a second and a second.

A center in a table.

It was a way a day, this made some sum. Suppose a cod liver a cod liver is an oil, suppose a cod liver oil is tunny, suppose a cod liver oil tunny is pressed suppose a cod liver oil tunny pressed is china and secret with a bestow a bestow reed, a reed to be a reed to be, in a reed to be.

Next to me next to a folder, next to a folder some waiter, next to a foldersome waiter and re letter and read her. Read her with her for less.

ROOMS

Act so that there is no use in a center. A wide action is not a width. A preparation is given to the ones preparing. They do not eat who mention silver and sweet. There was an occupation.

A whole center and a border make hanging a way of dressing. This which is not why there is a voice is the remains of an offering. There was no rental.

So the tune which is there has a little piece to play and the exercise is all there is of a fast. The tender and true that makes no width to hew is the time that there is question to adopt.

To begin the placing there is no wagon. There is no change lighter. It was done. And then the spreading, that was not accomplishing that needed standing and yet the time was not so difficult as they were not all in place. They had no change. They were not respected. They were that, they did it so much in the matter and this showed that that settlement was not condensed. It was spread there. Any change was in the ends of the center. A heap was heavy. There was no change.

Burnt and behind and lifting a temporary stone and lifting more than a drawer.

The instance of there being more is an instance of more. The shadow is not shining in the way there is a black line. The truth has come. There is a disturbance. Trusting to a baker's boy meant that there would be very much exchanging and anyway what is the use of a covering to a door. There is a use, they are double.

If the center has the place then there is distribution. That is natural. There is a contradiction and naturally returning there comes to be both sides and the center. That can be seen from the description.

The author of all that is in there behind the door and that is entering in the morning. Explaining darkening and expecting relating is all of a piece. The stove is bigger. It was of a shape that made no audience bigger and if the opening is assumed why should there not be kneeling. Any force which is bestowed on a floor shows rubbing. This is so nice and sweet and yet there comes the change, there comes the time to press more air. This does not mean the same as disappearance.

A little lingering lion and a chinese chair, all the handsome cheese which is stone, all of it and a choice, a choice of a blotter. If it is difficult to do it one way there is no place of similar trouble. None. The whole arrangement is established. The end of which is that there is a suggestion, a suggestion that there can be a different whiteness to a wall. This was thought.

A page to a corner means that the shame is no greater when the table is longer. A glass is of any height, it is higher, it is simpler and if it were placed there would not be any doubt.

Something that is an erection is that which stands and feeds and silences a tin which is swelling. This makes no diversion that is to say what can please exaltation, that which is cooking.

A shine is that which when covered changes permission. An enclosure blends with the same that is to say there is blending. A blend is that which holds no mice and this is not because of a floor it is because of nothing, it is not in a vision.

A fact is that when the place was replaced all was left that was stored and all was retained that would not satisfy more than another. The question is this, is it possible to suggest more to replace that thing. This question and this perfect denial does make the time change all the time.

The sister was not a mister. Was this a surprise. It was. The conclusion came when there was no arrangement. All the time that there was a question there was a decision. Replacing a casual acquaintance with an ordinary daughter does not make a son.

It happened in a way that the time was perfect and there was a growth of a whole dividing time so that where formerly there was no mistake there was no mistake now. For instance before when there was a separation there was waiting, now when there is separation there is the division between intending and departing. This made no more mixture than there would be if there had been no change.

A little sign of an entrance is the one that made it alike. If it were smaller it was not alike and it was so much smaller that a table was bigger. A table was much bigger, very much bigger. Changing that made nothing bigger, it did not make anything bigger littler, it did not hinder wood from not being used as leather. And this was so charming. Harmony is so essential. Is there pleasure when there is a passage, there is when every room is open. Every room is open when there are not four, there were there and surely there were four, there were two together. There is no resemblance.

A single speed, the reception of table linen, all the wonder of six little spoons, there is no exercise.

The time came when there was a birthday. Every day was no excitement and a birthday was added, it was added on Monday, this made the memory clear, this which was a speech showed the chair in the middle where there was copper.

Alike and a snail, this means Chinamen, it does there is no doubt that to be right is more than perfect there is no doubt and glass is confusing it confuses the substance which was of a color. Then came the time for discrimination, it came then and it was never mentioned it was so triumphant, it showed the whole bead that had a hole and should have a hole it showed the resemblance between silver.

Startling a starving husband is not disagreeable. The reason that nothing is hidden is that there is no suggestion of silence. No song is sad. A lesson is of consequence.

Blind and weak and organised and worried and betrothed and resumed and also asked to a fast and always asked to consider and never startled and not at all bloated, this which is no rarer than frequently is not so astonishing when hair brushing is added. There is quiet, there certainly is.

No eye glasses are rotten, no window is useless and yet if air will not come in there is a speech ready, there always is and there is no dimness, not a bit of it.

All along the tendency to deplore the absence of more has not been authorised. It comes to mean that with burning there is that pleasant state of stupifaction. Then there is a way of earning a living. Who is a man.

A silence is not indicated by any motion, less is indicated by a motion, more is not indicated it is enthralled. So sullen and so low, so much resignation, so much refusal and so much place for a lower and an upper, so much and yet more silence, why is not sleeping a feat why is it not and when is there some discharge when. There never is.

If comparing a piece that is a size that is recognised as not a size but a piece, comparing a piece with what is not recognised but what is used as it is held by holding, comparing these two comes to be repeated. Suppose they are put together, suppose that there is an interruption, supposing that beginning again they are not changed as to position, suppose all this and suppose that any five two of whom are not separating suppose that the five are not consumed. Is there an exchange, is there a resemblance to the sky which is admitted to be there and the stars which can be seen. Is there. That was a question. There was no certainty. Fitting a failing meant that any two were indifferent and yet they were all connecting that, they were all connecting that consideration. This did not determine rejoining a letter. This did not make letters smaller. It did.

The stamp that is not only torn but also fitting is not any symbol. It suggests nothing. A sack that has no opening suggests more and the loss is not commensurate. The season gliding and the torn hangings receiving mending all this shows an example, it shows the force of sacrifice and likeness and disaster and a reason.

The time when there is not the question is only seen when there is a shower. Any little thing is water.

There was a whole collection made. A damp cloth, an oyster, a single mirror, a manikin, a student, a silent star, a single spark, a little movement and the bed is made. This shows the disorder, it does, it shows more likeness than anything else, it shows the single mind that directs an apple. All the coats have a different shape, that does not mean that they differ in color, it means a union between use and exercise and a horse.

A plain hill, one is not that which is not white and red and green, a plain hill makes no sunshine, it shows that without a disturber. So the shape is there and the color and the outline and the miserable center, it is not very likely that there is a center, a hill is a hill and no hill is contained in a pink tender descender.

A can containing a curtain is a solid sentimental usage. The trouble in both eyes does not come from the same symmetrical carpet, it comes from there being no more disturbance than in little paper. This does show the teeth, it shows color.

A measure is that which put up so that it shows the length has a steel construction. Tidiness is not delicacy, it does not destroy the whole piece, certainly not it has been measured and nothing has been cut off and even if that has been lost there is a name, no name is signed and left over, not any space is fitted so that moving about is plentiful. Why is there so much resignation in a package, why is there rain, all the same the chance has come, there is no bell to ring.

A package and a filter and even a funnel, all this together makes a scene and supposing the question arises is hair curly, is it dark and dusty, supposing that question arises, is brushing necessary, is it, the whole special suddenness commences then, there is no delusion.

A cape is a cover, a cape is not a cover in summer, a cape is a cover and the regulation is that there is no such weather. A cape is not always a cover, a cape is not a cover when there is another, there is always something in that thing in establishing a disposition to put wetting where it will not do more harm. There is always that disposition and in a way there is some use in not mentioning changing and in establishing the temperature, there is some use in it as establishing all that lives dimmer freer and there is no dinner in the middle of everything. There is no such thing.

Why is a pale white not paler than blue, why is a connection made by a stove, why is the example which is mentioned not shown to be the same, why is there no adjustment between the place and the separate attention. Why is there a choice in gamboling. Why is there no necessary dull stable, why is there a single piece of any color, why is there that sensible silence. Why is there the resistance in a mixture, why is there no poster, why is there that in the window, why is there no suggester, why is there no window, why is there no oyster closer. Why is there a circular diminisher, why is there a bather, why is there no scraper, why is there a dinner, why is there a bell ringer, why is there a duster, why is there a section of a similar resemblance, why is there that scissor.

South, south which is a wind is not rain, does silence choke speech or does it not.

Lying in a conundrum, lying so makes the springs restless, lying so is a reduction, not lying so is arrangeable.

Releasing the oldest auction that is the pleasing some still renewing.

Giving it away, not giving it away, is there any difference. Giving it away. Not giving it away.

Almost very likely there is no seduction, almost very likely there is no stream, certainly very likely the height is penetrated, certainly certainly the target is cleaned. Come to sit, come to refuse, come to surround, come slowly and age is not lessening. The time which showed that was when there was no eclipse. All the time that rerenting was removal all that time there was breath. No breath is shadowed, no breath is painstaking and yet certainly what could be the use of paper, paper shows no disorder, it shows no desertion.

Why is there a difference between one window and

another, why is there a difference, because the curtain is shorter. There is no distaste in beefsteak or in plums or in gallons of milk water, there is no defiance in original piling up over a roof, there is no daylight in the evening, there is none there empty.

A tribune, a tribune does not mean paper, it means nothing more than cake, it means more sugar, it shows the state of lengthening any nose. The last spice is that which shows the whole evening spent in that sleep, it shows so that walking is an alleviation, and yet this astonishes everybody the distance is so sprightly. In all the time there are three days, those are not passed uselessly. Any little thing is a change that is if nothing is wasted in that cellar. All the rest of the chairs are established.

A success, a success is alright when there are there rooms and no vacancies, a success is alright when there is a package, success is alright anyway and any curtain is wholesale. A curtain diminishes and an ample space shows varnish.

One taste one tack, one taste one bottle, one taste one fish, one taste one barometer. This shows no distinguishing sign when there is a store.

Any smile is stern and any coat is a sample. Is there any use in changing more doors than there are committees. This question is so often asked that squares show that they are blotters. It is so very agreeable to hear a voice and to see all the signs of that expression.

Cadences, real cadences, real cadences and a quiet color. Careful and curved, cake and sober, all accounts and mixture, a guess at anything is righteous, should there be a call there would be a voice.

A line in life, a single line and a stairway, a rigid cook, no cook and no equator, all the same there is higher than that another evasion. Did that mean shame, it meant memory. Looking into a place that was hanging and was visible looking into this place and seeing a chair did that mean relief, it did, it certainly did not cause constipation and yet there is a melody that has white for a tune when there is straw color. This shows no face.

Star-light, what is star-light, star light is a little light that is not always mentioned with the sun, it is mentioned with the moon and the sun, it is mixed up with the rest of the time.

Why is the name changed. The name is changed because in the little space there is a tree, in some space there are no trees, in every space there is a hint of more, all this causes the decision.

Why is there education, there is education because the two tables which are folding are not tied together with a ribbon, string is used and string being used there is a necessity for another one and another one not being used to hearing shows no ordinary use of any evening and yet there is no disgrace in looking, none at all. This came to separate when there was simple selection of an entire preoccupation.

A curtain, a curtain which is fastened discloses mourning, this does not mean sparrows or elocution or ever a whole preparation, it means that there are ears and very often more much more altogether.

Climate, climate is not southern, a little glass, a bright winter, a strange supper an elastic tumbler, all this shows that the back is furnished and red which is red is a dark color. An example of this is fifteen years and a separation of regret.

China is not down when there are plates, lights are not ponderous and incalculable.

Currents, currents are not in the air and on the floor and in the door and behind it first. Currents do not show it plainer. This which is mastered has so thin a space to build it all that there is plenty of room and yet is it quarreling, it is not and the insistence is marked. A change is in a current and there is no habitable exercise.

A religion, almost a religion, any religion, a quintal in religion, a relying and a surface and a service in indecision and a creature and a question and a syllable in answer and more counting and no quarrel and a single scientific statement and no darkness and no question and an earned administration and a single set of sisters and an outline and no blisters and the section seeing yellow and the center having spelling and no solitude and no quaintness and yet solid quite so solid and the single surface centered and the question in the placard and the singularity, is there a singularity, and the singularity, why is there a question and the singularity why is the surface outrageous, why is it beautiful why is it not when there is no doubt, why is anything vacant, why is not disturbing a center no virtue, why is it when it is and why is it when it is and is and there is no doubt, there is no doubt that the singularity shows.

A climate, a single climate, all the time there is a single climate, any time there is a doubt, any time there is music that is to question more and more and there is no politeness, there is hardly any ordeal and certainly there is no table-cloth.

This is a sound and obligingness more obligingness leads to a harmony in hesitation.

A lake a single lake which is a pond and a little water any water which is an ant and no burning, not any burning, all this is sudden.

A canister that is the remains of furniture and a looking

glass and a bed-room and a larger size, all the stand is shouted and what is ancient is practical. Should the resemblance be so that any little cover is copied, should it be so that yards are measured, should it be so and there be a sin, should it be so then certainly a room is big enough when it is so empty and the corners are gathered together.

The change is mercenary that settles whitening the coloring and serving dishes where there is metal and making yellow any yellow every color in a shade which is expressed in a tray. This is a monster and awkward quite awkward and the little design which is flowered which is not strange and yet has visible writing, this is not shown all the time but at once, after that it rests where it is and where it is in place. No change is not needed. That does show design.

Excellent, more excellence is borrowing and slanting very slanting is light and secret and a recitation and emigration. Certainly shoals are shallow and nonsense more nonsense is sullen. Very little cake is water, very little cake has that escape.

Sugar any sugar, anger every anger, lover sermon lover, center no distractor, all order is in a measure.

Left over to be a lamp light, left over in victory, left over in saving, all this and negligence and bent wood and more even much more is not so exact as a pen and a turtle and even, certainly, and even a piece of the same experience as more.

To consider a lecture, to consider it well is so anxious and so much a charity and really supposing there is grain and if a stubble every stubble is urgent, will there not be a chance of legality. The sound is sickened and the price is purchased and golden what is golden, a clergyman, a single tax, a currency and an inner chamber.

Checking an emigration, checking it by smiling and

certainly by the same satisfactory stretch of hands that have more use for it than nothing, and mildly not mildly a correction, not mildly even a circumstance and a sweetness and a serenity. Powder, that has no color, if it did have would it be white.

A whole soldier any whole soldier has no more detail than any case of measles.

A bridge a very small bridge in a location and thunder, any thunder, this is the capture of reversible sizing and more indeed more can be cautious. This which makes monotony careless makes it likely that there is an exchange in principle and more than that, change in organisation.

This cloud does change with the movements of the moon and the narrow the quite narrow suggestion of the building. It does and then when it is settled and no sounds differ then comes the moment when cheerfulness is so assured that there is an occasion.

A plain lap, any plain lap shows that sign, it shows that there is not so much extension as there would be if there were more choice in everything. And why complain of more, why complain of very much more. Why complain at all when it is all arranged that as there is no more opportunity and no more appeal and not even any more clinching that certainly now some time has come.

A window has another spelling, it has f all together, it lacks no more then and this is rain, this may even be something else, at any rate there is no dedication in splendor. There is a turn of the stranger.

Catholic to be turned is to venture on youth and a section of debate, it even means that no class where each one over fifty is regular is so stationary that there are invitations.

A curving example makes righteous finger nails. This is the only object in secretion and speech.

To begin the same four are no more than were taller. The rest had a big chair and a surveyance a cold accumulation of nausea, and even more than that, they had a disappointment.

Nothing aiming is a flower, if flowers are abundant then they are lilac, if they are not they are white in the center.

Dance a clean dream and an extravagant turn up, secure the steady rights and translate more than translate the authority, show the choice and make no more mistakes than yesterday.

This means clearness, it means a regular notion of exercise, it means more than that, it means liking counting, it means more than that, it does not mean exchanging a line.

Why is there more craving than there is in a mountain. This does not seem strange to one, it does not seem strange to an echo and more surely is in there not being a habit. Why is there so much useless suffering. Why is there.

Any wet weather means an open window, what is attaching eating, anything that is violent and cooking and shows weather is the same in the end and why is there more use in something than in all that.

The cases are made and books, back books are used to secure tears and church. They are even used to exchange black slippers. They can not be mended with wax. They show no need of any such occasion.

A willow and no window, a wide place stranger, a wideness makes an active center.

The sight of no pussy cat is so different that a tobacco zone is white and cream.

A lilac, all a lilac and no mention of butter, not even bread and butter, no butter and no occasion, not even a silent resemblance, not more care than just enough haughty.

A safe weight is that which when it pleases is hanging. A safer weight is one more naughty in a spectacle. The best game is that which is shiny and scratching. Please a pease and a cracker and a wretched use of summer.

Surprise, the only surprise has no occasion. It is an ingredient and the section the whole section is one season.

A pecking which is petting and no worse than in the same morning is not the only way to be continuous often.

A light in the moon the only light is on Sunday. What was the sensible decision. The sensible decision was that notwithstanding many declarations and more music, not even notwithstanding the choice and a torch and a collection, notwithstanding the celebrating hat and a vacation and even more noise than cutting, notwithstanding Europe and Asia and being overbearing, not even notwithstanding an elephant and a strict occasion, not even withstanding more cultivation and some seasoning, not even with not drowning and with the ocean being encircling, not even with more likeness and any cloud, not even with terrific sacrifice of pedestrianism and a special resolution, not even more likely to be pleasing. The care with which the rain is wrong and the green is wrong and the white is wrong, the care with which there is a chair and plenty of breathing. The care with which there is incredible justice and likeness, all this makes a magnificent asparagus and also a fountain.

FACSIMILE IMAGES

The two sides of this strip of paper (pages 79 and 81), torn from the manuscript notebook containing "Objects," list twenty-two corrections in Stein's hand, keyed to page and line numbers in the first edition. *Yale Collection of American Literature, Beinecke Rare Book and Manuscript Library, Yale University.*

The two sides of this strip of paper (pages 79 and 81), torn from the manuscript notebook containing "Objects," list twenty-two corrections in Stein's hand, keyed to page and line numbers in the first edition. *Yale Collection of American Literature, Beinecke Rare Book and Manuscript Library, Yale University.*

On the opening page of Donald Sutherland's copy of the first edition, Stein adds the letter S in the text and writes "surely any s is welcome" in the margin. She does not strike the prefix to "unwelcome" in the text, and this edition follows the manuscript and other sources in retaining it. *Special Collections Department, University of Colorado Boulder Libraries.*

A CARAFE, THAT IS A BLIND GLASS.

A kind in glass and a cousin, a spectacle and nothing strange a single hurt color and an arrangement in a system to pointing. All this and not ordinary, not unordered in not resembling. The difference is spreading.

GLAZED GLITTER.

Nickel, what is nickel, it is originally rid of a cover. The change in that is that red weakens an hour. The change has come. There is no search. But there is, there is that hope and that interpretation and sometime, surely any is unwelcome, sometime there is breath and there will be a sinecure and charming very charming is that clean and cleansing. Certainly glittering is handsome and convincing.

There is no gratitude in mercy and in medicine. There can be breakages in Japanese. That is no programme. That is no color chosen. It was chosen yesterday, that showed spitting and perhaps washing and polishing. It certainly showed no obligation and perhaps if borrowing is not natural there is some use in giving.

A SUBSTANCE IN A CUSHION.

The change of color is likely and a difference a very little difference is prepared. Sugar is not a vegetable.

(9)

Stein wrote this apparently unique inscription on the rear paste-down page in Donald Sutherland's copy of the first edition: "the concentration and the long struggle between ~~sound~~ sight sound and wide. and when it all came out so strangely." *Special Collections Department, University of Colorado Boulder Libraries.*

the consultation and
the long struggle
between ... eight word
... and ...
came out so
strongly.

A NOTE ON THE TEXT

by Seth Perlow

The corrected, centennial edition of Gertrude Stein's *Tender Buttons: Objects, Food, Rooms* collates previous versions of the book in order to establish a text that reflects the author's intentions as accurately as possible and corrects errors found in all existing versions. This note provides a brief history of *Tender Buttons* and describes the sources and methods that informed this edition.

Stein began writing the vignettes that would become *Tender Buttons* in the summer of 1912, while traveling in Spain. She had apparently completed the work when, in February 1914, the poet Donald Evans wrote her in Paris to ask if his private New York City press, Claire Marie, might publish some of her plays. In lieu of the plays, Stein sent Evans a three-part text titled "Food, Rooms, Objects." Evans established the standard order by moving "Objects" to the front, and Stein provided the general title, *Tender Buttons*, at his request. Evans sent Stein a publishing contract in March 1914, and in an accompanying letter he explained that sending page proofs to Stein in Paris would make it impossible to bring out the book before the end of May. By June, Evans warned, book reviewers in New York City would have quit for the summer, and *Tender Buttons* might go unnoticed. Stein agreed to leave the proofing to Evans, but her later corrections to the first edition indicate that she did not find his work satisfactory.

Claire Marie published the first edition of *Tender Buttons* in May 1914, printing 1,000 copies clad in yellow paper-covered boards with a circular green title paste-on. The book is fairly small, about 7" tall and 5" wide, and its ample margins surround an even smaller printed area. The book's first run was sufficiently limited and its renown sufficiently wide that *transition*, the Parisian literary magazine edited by Eugene Jolas, reprinted the full text in Issue 4, 1928, apparently working from the first edition. Since then, *Tender Buttons* has entered the public domain and appeared in a wide array of editions and collections. Although the work's brevity makes it more approachable, anthologies that include it often cannot reproduce the first edition's elegant spareness; the most common freestanding editions, meanwhile, pay little attention to formatting. None provides a reliable version of the text. This edition returns *Tender Buttons* to its original compact, freestanding form, and it is intended to be as accessible to casual readers as it is reliable for more serious students of Stein's writing.

The present text is based on comparisons among Stein's manuscript, a typescript prepared by Stein's partner Alice B. Toklas, the first edition, and two sets of corrections and revisions in Stein's hand. The manuscript and typescript are held at the Beinecke Rare Book and Manuscript Library, Yale University. The manuscript spans three notebooks, each about 8" tall and 6" wide, clad in black leather, and each containing one section of *Tender Buttons*. The letter "O" is scratched onto the front cover of the "Objects" notebook, "Fo" onto the "Food" notebook, and "Ro" onto the slimmer "Rooms" notebook. The notebooks are ruled horizontally, but Stein turned them sideways, making space for fewer, longer lines per page. She began by writing on each recto page, and when she had thus reached the end of a notebook, she flipped it and worked back to the front, writing on verso pages. Only the "Rooms" notebook is filled entirely. The notebooks do not indicate the order in which they were written or should be printed. The typescript, meanwhile, appears on single sides of standard typing paper, bound in a volume with other Stein typescripts; here "Rooms" appears first, followed by "Objects" and then "Food." The typescript bears two conflicting paginations. A typed series in the upper-right corner begins anew at the start of each section. Handwritten notes in the manuscript key it to these typed numbers, such that "/ [2]" in the manuscript indicates the start of the second page of typescript for that section. A second, handwritten pagination at the top- and bottom-right of each page runs continuously through the full typescript. Variances between the Beinecke typescript and the first edition suggest that Donald Evans worked from another, slightly different typescript, now lost.

The Stein collection at the Beinecke Library also includes a strip of paper torn from the manuscript notebooks, upon which Stein wrote 22 corrections to the first edition. Facsimiles of this strip appear on pages 78-81 of this edition. All but one of these corrections are corroborated in Stein's emendations to a copy of the first edition that belonged to the late literary critic Donald Sutherland, now held at the Norlin Library, University of Colorado Boulder. The history of the Sutherland copy is uncertain, but the corrections are clearly in Stein's hand. Sutherland fought in Europe during World War II, and Stein likely gave him this corrected copy at the end of the war, when he visited her in Paris. (Sutherland's wartime letters to his wife, archived at the Auraria Library, University of Colorado Denver, indicate he visited Stein before returning to the U.S.) In addition to the corrections matching those in the Beinecke collection, the Sutherland copy includes a unique inscription Stein wrote on the rear paste-down page. Pages 82-85 of this edition provide facsimiles of one corrected page from the Sutherland copy and of this previously unpublished note. Perhaps commenting on the composition of *Tender Buttons* itself, this strange inscription reads, "the concentration and the long struggle between ~~sound~~ sight sound and wide. and when it all came out so strangely."

Most editions of *Tender Buttons* follow either the typescript or the first edition, but Stein's notes indicate that neither fairly reflects her intentions for the book. Although the first edition does contain some errors not present in the typescript, Stein's corrections do not simply reconcile the first edition to the typescript. Rather, several corrections address errors present in both the first edition and the typescript, bringing the text into accordance with the manuscript. Without Stein's oversight, therefore, Donald Evans could not possibly have avoided many of the errors Stein would subsequently correct, for the typescript from which he worked likely contained these errors already.

.

This edition arbitrates a total of 137 variances in matters of wording, spelling, punctuation, and formatting. In general, the manuscript is given preference, but Stein's corrections to the first edition are preferred where applicable. The two sets of corrections are detailed and matched, so Stein took great care in proofing the first edition after its appearance. When there is uncertainty about a variance, therefore, I have given the corrected first edition equal weight and sought consensus among the manuscript, typescript, and corrected first edition. I have also compared these primary materials with one recent edition of *Tender Buttons*, the version appearing in the Library of America collection of Stein's *Writings 1903–1932*, which claims the Beinecke typescript as its source but differs from the typescript in some instances.

Formatting decisions generally follow cues from the manuscript and typescript rather than the first edition. For example, subheadings in this edition are centered between the margins, in accordance with the manuscript and typescript. The first edition aligns subheadings against the left margin. Likewise, this edition follows the typescript by using em-spaces to separate items in the list that opens "Food." The first edition separates items with semicolons (and places such semicolons erroneously). Other formatting cues are taken from the first edition, including the fairly wide margins and minimal indentation of the first line of each paragraph. In one case I have sought compromise on a formatting question. The manuscript and typescript set subsection headings in sentence case, but this makes them difficult to distinguish from the main text. The first edition sets subsection headings in block capitals, but these efface Stein's decisions about capitalization. This edition sets subsection headings in small capitals but uses large capitals for letters Stein capitalized in the manuscript—thus distinguishing subsection headings from the main text while preserving a difference between majuscule and minuscule letters.

This edition settles 72 variances in spelling. Of these, 35 negotiate differences between British and American conventions. Evans preferred the British "centre," but this edition follows the manuscript and typescript in using "center." Similarly, the typescript prefers "colour," but this edition follows the manuscript and first edition in using "color." Other recurring words, such as "authorised," follow British conventions here and in the source materials. Many of the remaining 37 orthographic variances alter the wording, and several resolve difficulties with Stein's handwriting. For instance, where the typescript and all extant editions read "woolen," the manuscript shows that Stein overwrote the l with a d, spelling "wooden." Twelve notes on spelling appear in Stein's corrections to the first edition. Four variances in spelling change words from singular to plural or vice versa; seven correct simple misspellings. In three cases, the final vowel is returned to "potatoe" and in one case to "tomatoe," in accordance with the manuscript and typescript; the first and other editions mistake these antiquated spellings for errors.

Twenty variances concern the recovery, removal,

or rearrangement of a whole word or phrase. In seven cases, a single word is recovered; in four a word is removed. In three cases, a phrase of two or more words is recovered. Two of these recovered phrases are absent in the first edition but present in the manuscript and typescript; one of the two appears in Stein's corrections as well. The third is a marginal note appearing only in the manuscript; it is included in the List of Variances but not in the text. In one case, the order of words in a phrase is rearranged; this edition follows the manuscript and first edition in preferring "it is" where the typescript reads "is it." Here and elsewhere, the first edition's agreement with the manuscript but not the typescript suggests Evans worked from a different typescript. Two phrases previously formatted as part of the main text are now set as subsection headings, and one paragraph break is removed. In two cases a phrase is removed. The first is a phrase struck through in the manuscript and absent in the first edition, but it appears in the typescript and its dependent editions. The second removed phrase is a subtitle, "Studies in Description," which Stein placed below the "Food" heading in the manuscript. In the same letter to Donald Evans where she provides the title, *Tender Buttons*, she also makes clear that she had considered "Studies in Description" as a subtitle for the entire work but that it should be omitted, in favor of the three section headings, "Food, Rooms, Objects." This discarded phrase's only appearance in the first edition is on a rear flyleaf, where an advertisement for Claire Marie's list in Belles-Lettres includes *Tender Buttons*, describing it as "Studies in Description by Gertrude Stein." The discarded subtitle also persists in the typescript, below the heading for "Food," and it appears there in editions based on the typescript.

Forty variances concern punctuation, including the addition or removal of hyphens, commas, periods, umlauts, and in one case, quotation marks. As usual, this edition seeks consensus among the manuscript, typescript, and first edition but, in cases of uncertainty, gives preference to the manuscript. Twenty-nine punctuation issues correct errors in the first edition, eight of which also appear in the typescript. Of the remaining eleven variances in punctuation, four diverge from the typescript but not the manuscript or first edition; one from the Library of America edition but not the typescript on which it is based; one from the manuscript and typescript; and five from the manuscript alone.

Last but not least, five of the variances addressed here concern capitalization of letters. Two of these depart from the manuscript. In one case, the manuscript lacks a capital letter after a full stop, and in the other, the manuscript provides a capital mid-sentence, likely to clarify spelling. Of the three remaining variances in capitalization, one corrects a word mistakenly capitalized in the typescript. Another capitalizes "Japanese," following the manuscript and first edition but not the typescript. The last sets "chinese" in lower case, in accordance with the manuscript and typescript but not the first edition.

This project began by chance, when I learned about Donald Sutherland's copy of *Tender Buttons* and its 21 corrections—a new discovery for me but not for Stein scholars. I hoped at first to bring out an edition of *Tender Buttons* that would incorporate these corrections and that might approximate the distinctive, spare form of the first edition. To my surprise, research for this project revealed over 100 additional variances affecting all extant versions of the text, from the original manuscript to the most recent anthologies. I hope that by resolving these errors and inconsistencies, this edition of *Tender Buttons* provides a durable and reliable version of this wonderful book.

LIST OF VARIANCES

This list records all variances addressed in the present edition with the exception of global changes mentioned above, such as reversions to American spelling. Each entry lists the sources followed herein, the sources contravened, and the contra-indicated gloss of the text. Further explanation appears when necessary. The following abbreviations are used: M for the manuscript of *Tender Buttons*; T for the typescript; F for the first edition; B for Stein's corrections at the Beinecke Library; S for Stein's corrections in Donald Sutherland's copy of the first edition; and L for the Library of America edition. Because B and S represent lists of corrections and not full texts of *Tender Buttons*, they do not appear in every entry. Entries are listed by page number, followed by a decimal, and line number (e.g., 12.2 indicates page 12, line 2).

Objects

9.1: Per M, F, L. Contra T, "Objects." The period is omitted and, per F, the heading set in block capitals.

11.6: Per M. Contra T, L, "Glazed Glitter". F sets subheadings in block capitals.

11.10–11: Per M, B, S, T. Contra F, L, "surely any is unwelcome". A marginal note in S reads "surely any s is welcome" but does not strike "unwelcome" in the text.

12.2: Per M, B, S, L. Contra T, F, "very clean".

12.5: Per M, B. Contra T, F, L, "use in feather".

12.8: Per F, L. Contra M, T, "tassle".

14.5: Per M. Contra T, F, L, "rose-wood".

14.13: Per T, F, L. Contra M, "lining, and". In M a comma appears but is struck through.

14.22: Per M, T, L. Contra F, where a paragraph break appears after "harder".

16.17: Per T, F, L. Following this paragraph in M is a parenthetical note, "(go on with boxes — then cig case)". Stein likely paused writing here; cigarettes appear in the next paragraph.

19.12–13: Per M, T, B, S, L. Contra F, which omits "if the event is overtaken,".

21.8: Per M, T, F. Contra L, "has a use". A hand-correction to "had" appears in T, but L does not follow the correction.

22.1: Per T, F, L. Contra M, "More", omitting the period.

23.6: Per M, F. Contra T, L, "culture is japanese".

25.3: Per M. Contra T, F, L, "woolen object".

26.5: Per M, T, L. Contra F, "foot-path".

27.10–11: Per M, T. Contra F, L, "watermelon".

27.19: Per M, B, S. Contra T, F, L, "noon and moon and moon".

27.26: Per M, T, B, S, L. Contra F, "leading mention nothing".

29.19: Per M, B, S. Contra T, F, L, "ballon and".

29.20: Per M, B, S. Contra T, F, L, "sizer of talks".

30.10: Per M, T, B, S, L. Contra F, "again, back it".

31.5: Per M, T, B, S. Contra F, L, "Excellent".

31.8: Per M, B, S. Contra T, F, L, "Aider, why aider".

Food

33.1: Per M, F, L. Contra T, "Food." The period is omitted and, per F, the heading set in block capitals.

33.1: Per F. Contra M, T, L, which include "Studies in Description" as a subtitle. A note in Stein's hand, archived with B, indicates this phrase should be omitted.

34.1–9: Per T, L. Contra F, which separates elements in the list with semicolons. Contra M, which arranges elements in four columns. M and F give the list its own page, but in T and L it shares a page with the section heading, "Food". M, T, and L set the list in sentence case, F in block capitals.

34.2: Per F, L. Contra M, T, "tails,".

34.3: Per M, T, L. Contra F, which sets "single; fish" as two items.

34.8: Per M, T, L. Contra F, which sets "cocoa; and clear soup and oranges and oat-meal" as two items.

34.9: Per T, F, L. Contra M, "artichoke,".

35.19: Per M, F. Contra T, L, "pliant." In M, Stein corrects "pliant" to "plain", but T does not reflect this change. B and S do not correct "plain" to "plaint", indicating that "plain" is the proper gloss and that F is based on a typescript other than T.

35.24: Per M, T, L. Contra F, "reëstablishment".

36.25: Per T, F, L. Contra M, "principle".

36.30: Per M. Contra T, F, L, "is obtrusive suppose it is".

37.4: Per F, L. Contra M, T, "symetry".

37.11: Per M, F, L. Contra T, "is it not assiduous".

37.30: Per M, T, F. Contra L, "That choice".

40.17: Per M, T, L. Contra F, "reëstablishment".

41.16: Per M, T, L. Contra F, "makes a shunning".

41.21: Per M, T, L. Contra F, "tomato".

42.1: Per M, T, L. Contra F, "even makes makes no more".

42.2: Per M, B, S. Contra T, F, L, "suggestion in vanity".

42.26: Per M, B, S. Contra T, F, L, "imitation succeed".

43.7: Per M, T, L. Contra F, "tea-cups".

43.21: Per F, L. Contra M, T, "pursuasion".

45.26: Per T, F, L. Contra M, which breaks "crest / fallen" across two manuscript pages.

47.1: Per M, B, S. Contra T, F, L, "basting undip".

47.3: Per M, T, L. Contra F, "twenty-four".

47.8: Per M. Contra T, F, L, "altogether".

48.17: Per M, T, L. Contra F, "shake, potato".

48.17: Per M, T, L. Contra F, "potato and".

49.7: Per T, F, L. Contra M, "Lunch", omitting the period.

49.14: Per M, T, L. Contra F, "natural, and".

49.17: Per T, F, L. Contra M, "real beds". In T "beds" is hand-corrected to "beads".

49.18: Per M. Contra T, F, L, "that bees more than".

50.14: Per M, T, L. Contra F, "Peanuts".

50.20: Per M, T, L. Contra F, "egg-plant".

51.3: Per M, T, L. Contra F, "today".

52.16: Per M, T, B, S, L. Contra F, "little keep a strange".

52.21: Per M, T, B, S, L. Contra F, "between a lounge".

53.20: Per M, F. Contra T, L, "cross a crescent".

54.2: Per M, T, L. Contra F, "have a skip".

54.18: Per M, F. Contra T, L, "Mean. Why. Potatoes.". In M "Why." is struck through.

54.18: Per M, T. Contra F, L, "Potato".

55.16: Per F, L. Contra M, T, "razor, Ridiculous pudding". Stein appears to have capitalized "ridiculous" to clarify her handwriting; the preceding punctuation in M is a comma.

56.2: Per M, T, L. Contra F, "fit sun sat in shed".

56.5: Per M, T, L. Contra F, "sell never never be".

56.12: Per M, T, L. Contra F, "measure".

56.12–13: Per M, T, L. Contra F, "yet all the one".

56.17–18: Per F, L. Contra M, T, "be no so. all to be".

59.1–2: Per M, T. Contra F, L, which set "Cocoa and clear soup and oranges and oat-meal." as part of the previous subsection. M contains a parenthetical note labeling this phase "(Title)". T runs the phrase together with the previous paragraph but contains a handwritten pilcrow indicating a break. In F the phrase begins a new paragraph, but not in L. No previous edition has set the phrase as a subsection heading, a decision further supported by its appearance in the list at the start of "Food".

59.4–5: Ibid.

Rooms

61.1: Per M, F, L. Contra T, "Rooms." The period is omitted and, per F, the heading set in block capitals.

63.8-9: Per M, T, L. Contra F, "to play. and the".

64.4: Per M, T, F. Contra L, "It was a shape".

64.4: Per M. Contra T, F, L, "bigger if the opening".

64.10: Per M, T, L. Contra F, "Chinese chair".

65.1: Per M, F. Contra T, L, "more to replace anything than there is to replace that thing". The phrase "anything than there is to replace" is struck through in M, absent in F, but present in T, suggesting again that F is based on a typescript other than T.

66.6: Per M, T, L. Contra F, "whole head".

66.16: Per M, T, L. Contra F, "eye-glasses".

66.21: Per M. Contra T, F, L, "stupefication".

66.27: Per M, T, F. Contra L, "silence why".

68.1: Per M, T, B, S, L. Contra F, "centre. it is". The full stop is corrected to a comma and, as throughout, the spelling Americanized.

68.31: Per M, B, S. Contra T, F, L, "middle of anything".

69.27: Per M, B, S. Contra T, F, L, "resenting".

69.28: Per M, T, B, S, L. Contra F, "was breadth".

71.8: Per M. Contra T, F, L, "star-light is a little".

71.21: Per M, T, L. Contra F, "entire pre-occupation".

71.23: Per M, B, S. Contra T, F, L, "even a whole".

71.24–25: Per M, T, L. Contra F, "often much more altogether".

72.20–21: Per M, T, L. Contra F, "when it is and there is no doubt".

72.25: Per M, T. Contra F, L, "no tablecloth".

72.31: Per M, F. Contra T, L, "cannister".

72.31–73.1: Per M, T, L. Contra F, "looking-glass".

73.1: Per M, F. Contra T, L, "bed room".

74.12: Per M, T, L. Contra F, "organization".

74.25: Per M. Contra T, F, L, "has "f" all together". Quotation marks appear nowhere else in the text. Stein's insertion of a single letter without them in B and S further supports their removal here (cf 11.10–11).

75.1: Per M. Contra T, F, L, "finger-nails".

75.3: Per M, T, L. Contra F, "To being the same".

76.17: Per M, T, F. Contra L, "not even withstanding an elephant".

76.19: Per M, T, B, S, L. Contra F, "not even with drowning".

76.27: Per M. Contra T, F, L, "asparagus, and also".

AFTERWORD

by Juliana Spahr

That *Tender Buttons* is revolutionary has been said many times. What is meant by this is something about how it is made, something about its aesthetics, not something about its political affiliations. It is a work, the story goes, that broke apart the aesthetic conventions of Literature, of nineteenth-century literature, of realism, of literary nationalism. It is often said to be *sui generis*. And a hundred years later, there is no denying that *Tender Buttons* is a major work. One that continues to do some breaking.

This is a lot of weight to put on such a slender work. *Tender Buttons* is, give or take, a mere 15,000 words. It was first published in 1914 by Claire Marie in a print run of around 1,000 copies. The original edition was seventy-eight pages, spare, with no illustrations and a restrained typography. While it was the first book by Stein that was not self-published, Claire Marie was still a very modest press that published mainly friends and friends of friends, edited by the decadent poet Donald Evans. It is hard to imagine a less presumptuous arrival for an aesthetic revolution.

Tender Buttons is written in what one might call prose, the word that tends to get used for sentences that do not follow realist conventions and instead have poetry's associational drive but not its line breaks. While it uses fairly simple language in that there are few words that require a dictionary, it indulges in a lot of grammatical variations. It runs on: "Callous is something that hardening leaves behind what will be soft if there is a genuine interest in their being present as many girls as men." It hangs fire in fragments: "Roast potatoes for." It frequently indulges in a fragmented listing: "An elegant use of foliage and grace and a little piece of white cloth and oil." At moments it even manages to run on in fragments: "Cold pails, cold with joy no joy." It seems often to have a definitional desire. But it is a complicated desire. Things get defined all the time. "Sugar," for instance, is first "A peck a small piece." And then Stein follows with a list of negatives, "not privately overseen, not at all not a slice, not at all crestfallen and open, not at all mounting and chaining and evenly surpassing, all the bidding comes to tea." Sometimes all is grammatically set up for a definition but the words seem to have only the vaguest relation to each other: "Nickel, what is nickel, it is originally rid of a cover"; "Rhubarb is susan not susan not seat in bunch toys not wild and laughable not in little places not in neglect and vegetable not in fold coal age not please"; "A blind agitation is manly and uttermost."

The work seems to be at its most obvious a possible description of a domestic space. But it is unclear where this domestic space is located. There is no hint of a nation state and only the vaguest hint that it is the turn of the century. It is, however, clearly a bourgeois interior, full of objects such as seltzer bottles, dresses, hats, umbrellas, tables, books, with a kitchen full of the proteins and the luxuries, roastbeef, chickens, pastry, and cocoa. There is no obvious narrator. And while the domestic space is often seen as a female space, and there are some moments where gender shows up ("Mildred's umbrella"; "A long dress"; "A petticoat"; "A little called Pauline"; etc.), the space does not feel particularly gendered. There is also no sign of domestic labor, no sign of who is doing the cooking, the cleaning.

So this is not a literature of national identity nor of landscape. It is not a literature of philosophical questioning nor of transcendence nor a call to arms. Neither is it a *bildungsroman*, nor an exploration of personal or cultural identity. It might be a sort of novel of manners in reverse: one that shows the space of the novel of manners and not the niceties and aggressions and passions and conversations between humans that are the novel of manners. That this space is so fractured, so broken, seems suggestive of something. And it seems safe to say that this something might possibly be about daily life. But what *Tender Buttons* wants to say beyond this is an open question.

It is tempting to say that *Tender Buttons* says something feminist, something queer, something opposed to those big modernist epics such as T. S. Eliot's "The Waste Land" or Ezra Pound's *The Cantos*, works that were being written at the time Stein was writing hers.[1] Many before me have said things about Stein as possibly a feminist writer. And not without good reason. Stein was someone who, to her credit, wrote a play about Susan B. Anthony in which she called her *The Mother of Us All*, and she also wrote the queer, erotic celebration of female bodies that is *Lifting Belly*.[2] But Stein's politics make little consistent sense. She was, after all, a Jewish lesbian interested in the work of Otto Weininger, the author of the anti-Semitic, homophobic, and mysoginist *Sex and Character*.[3]

What makes *Tender Buttons* aesthetically revolutionary makes some love it. And some hate it. And still others love to hate it. It received a lot of attention from various newspapers shortly after its publication in 1914. As Stein wrote in the voice of Toklas that she uses in *The Autobiography of Alice B. Toklas*: "it was a very charming little book and Gertrude Stein was enormously pleased, and it, as every one knows, had an enormous influence on all young writers and started off columnists in the newspapers of the whole country on their long campaign of ridicule. I must say that when the columnists are really funny, and they quite often are, Gertrude Stein chuckles and reads them aloud to me."[4] Some of this attention was positive: "Those who are avid for the literature of tomorrow will find great satisfaction in this book," said the *Buffalo Times*.[5] Some of it not: "What?" said the *Boston Herald*.[6] *Tender Buttons* was also frequently parodied at the time. Don Marquis regularly published parodies of Stein in his column for the New York newspaper *The Evening Sun* in 1914–1915. Stein parodies also showed up in the pages of *The Atlantic* during this same period.

There has also been a long debate about how to read *Tender Buttons*, about what sort of meaning to ascribe to its chairs, its chickens, its pastries. One common way that these readers find their way around the atypicality of *Tender Buttons* is to read the book as a code that can be broken. Marjorie Perloff speaks of the "synecdochic riddling poetry of *Tender Buttons*."[7] And many have attempted to enumerate these riddles and then to propose a possible meaning. It has been said that it presents "a woman-centered, revisionary spirituality."[8]

That there is "increasingly explicit" dildo imagery, and also that it is about oral sex with a circumcised penis, and then there is a clitoris that is rubbed with a rubber cock too.[9] Others argue it is about a woman's nipples. No, still others reply, it is about the early buddings of a plant.[10] That Stein was stoned when she wrote it has been suggested more than once, often followed by a reference to the recipe for "haschich fudge" in Alice B. Toklas's cookbook.[11] Some of these readings are excellent, fun. One aspect of the many possible pleasures that might arise from reading Stein is reading how others read Stein. I am especially partial to William Gass's essays. He is the one who insists *Tender Buttons* is full of dildos in "Gertrude Stein and the Geography of the Sentence," and the essay is hilarious, bawdy, even if not entirely convincing. The exchange of letters between Paul Padgette and Virgil Thompson in the *New York Review of Books* in the 1970s on the nipples versus early buddings of a plant interpretation is also lovely and does not disappoint. These readings are also to be appreciated for the way they make clear that it is not that *Tender Buttons* is unreadable, not that it is too difficult, but rather that it is an optimistic demonstration of how possible it is to read, of how, luckily, our imaginations are impossible to regulate and restrict, of how it might not be possible to find something unreadable. But that the deciphering does not hold, or that each of these readings feels so provisional to the work as a whole, has to be part of the point. *Tender Buttons*, a book always in the process of being read over and over.

And yet if there is anything that can be said about

the reception of Stein over the century, "contradictory" might be the best descriptor. In her time, she was a classic example of that author that one uses to show one's mettle as a critic by how well one argues for or against. Early on, every argument made in defense of the work also seems to be used to attack it. Over and over. So Edith Sitwell defends Stein as "bringing back life to our language by what appears, at first, to be an anarchic process."[12] Max Eastman attacks in the libertarian journal *The Freeman*, using her work as a prominent example of what he calls "the non-communicative art," or "mumbo-jumbo," and as he does this he indulges in terms that might today be used by to describe an anticiv anarchist; Stein is "part of that general surrender of mental and moral integrity to crude primitive and unilluminated states of passion which threatens our whole Graeco-Christian civilization with ruin. I think this will seem quite obvious to future historians if history survives."[13] Laura Riding defends the primitive possibility, perhaps, in an article that again uses the word anarchism: "Gertrude Stein, by combining the functions of critic and poet and taking everything around her very literally and many things for granted which others have not been naïve enough to take so, has done what everyone else has been ashamed to do. No one but she has been willing to be as ordinary, as simple, as primitive, as stupid, as barbaric as successful barbarism demands."[14] In 1931, she is important enough to get her own chapter in something like Edmund Wilson's *Axel's Castle*, even though he calls her work "absolutely unintelligible even to a sympathetic reader."[15]

Yet by the 1950s, Stein seems to fall out of the discussion. She is not a crucial part of the canon of American literature as it is taught in higher education until late in the twentieth century. Astrid Lorange in her study of Stein, talking about the December 1978 issue of the zine *L=A=N=G=U=A=G=E*—this issue had a forum on *Tender Buttons* that featured a number of now-major U.S. writers such as Michael Davidson, Bob Perelman, and Jackson Mac Low—claims that "December 1978 figures as a significant moment in which Stein is reintroduced to critical scholarship in the context of radical poetics."[16] She might be overstating the importance of this fairly modest zine, but she is right in intent in that, in the last half of the century, Stein begins to be read again. And not just by contemporary poets but also by scholars. She eventually enters the academy. First as a feminist writer in Marianne DeKoven's *A Different Language: Gertrude Stein's Experimental Language* and Shari Benstock's *Women of the Left Bank: Paris 1900-1940* in the 1980s.[17] Then as an aesthetic innovator. Perloff, who in her 1983 *The Poetics of Indeterminancy: Rimbaud to Cage* establishes the reigning methodology of close reading avant-garde works with a devoted formal attention, is hugely influential in defining a certain series of conventions about how "radical" writing is read in the academy, and repeatedly in her work mentions Stein as "the most radical American writer of the early twentieth century."[18] At another moment, she claims "Stein is *sui generis*."[19] *Tender Buttons* might easily be thought of as the work that establishes the narrative of Stein the innovator. And the book has a significant impact on contemporary U.S. writing. It is hard to imagine Language writing happening without its influence.

There has been so much attention to what is happening in the room, in the book itself, that there has not been that much attention to what is happening outside of the room of *Tender Buttons*. Although *Tender Buttons* was published in the U.S. and was written by someone who is considered to be a U.S. writer, it was written by a writer who lived in a room in Paris at the turn of the century. I say this even as there is nothing marked as necessarily Parisian or even French in the work. It is not that *Tender Buttons* is about a particular national interior. *Tender Buttons* has little to do with nationalism. Later a nationalist, even jingoist, Stein will appear. This is the Stein whose *Four Saints in Three Acts*, as adapted by Virgil Thomson, was part of the State Department's "Masterpieces of the Twentieth Century" festival and had Leontyne Price placed in the lead by the Secretary General of the Congress for Cultural Freedom (an anticommunist advocacy group with close ties to the CIA), the Stein who wrote defenses of patriotism and claimed "there is something in this native land business and you cannot get away from it."[20] But this Stein would not show up until after the wars. The Stein, though, of *Tender Buttons* was writing in the Paris of the turn of the twentieth century, which at the time was something multivalent and resonant, multifaceted in its social relations. It was the world capital of culture. And the center of empire. And it was unusually transnational, full of various immigrants. Raymond

Williams calls Paris at the time "a complexity and a sophistication of social relations, supplemented in the most important cases . . . by exceptional liberties of expression."[21] These social relations were complex in some ways and not in others. While Paris often served for some as a refuge from U.S. racism, many found the rumor of a color-blind France to be a myth. In this, the unusually transnational center of empire that was Paris was still like most other places.

But whether Paris at the time was a new social experiment or an old one that was under new and reformatory pressures, Stein is one of its many immigrants, even if a fairly privileged one with an inheritance. She is a writer who very literally comes out of the flexible and complex migration patterns of Europeans and Americans before World War I. Stein, as she points out in the voice of Toklas in *The Autobiography of Alice B. Toklas*, had no mother tongue; she "prattled in german and then in french" before she read and spoke English.[22] When Stein was three years old, her family moved first to Vienna and then to Paris, so she learned French and German before she learned English. They then moved back to the U.S., settling in Oakland, California. After a childhood and a young adulthood in the U.S., she moved in 1902 to London, eventually settling in Paris the next year. *Tender Buttons* was written during the first decade of Stein's voluntary exile.

And yet despite her early polylingualism and then her later immersion in polylingual Paris, Stein more or less writes only in English, with mainly small, everyday words. This is one of the obvious differences between her work and that of fellow aesthetic innovators Eliot and Pound. But at the same time, it makes sense to see her work as part of this intensely globalizing culture and to see Stein as a writer who looked around and saw a world suddenly full of many sorts of languages from all over the place, a writer who embraced this by bringing all sorts of nonstandard language patterns into English. Concerns with language, with fluency, with an immigrant relation to culture and language are throughout Stein's work. As she writes in *Tender Buttons*, "It is so very agreeable to hear a voice and to see all the signs of that expression. Cadences, real cadences, real cadences and a quiet color." She is a lover of the cross-lingual homonym, the pun, and the homophonic translation. Or as she orders in *Tender Buttons*, "secure the steady rights and translate more than translate the authority, show the choice."

But also, not just a room, not just a room in Paris. . . . When Virginia Woolf writes about this time, she does it like this: "On or about December 1910 human character changed."[23] She is at this moment telling a story about the origins of the aesthetic revolution that is modernism. She is said to be referring to Roger Fry's November 1910 exhibition "Manet and the Post-Impressionists," which showcased work by Cézanne, Gauguin, Manet, Matisse, and Van Gogh. But Fry's exhibit goes unmentioned by Woolf, and in the essay she locates November 1910 as when "All human relations have shifted—those between masters and servants, husbands and wives, parents and children."[24] And this, she asserts, changes literature. In 1910, she continues, "the smashing and the crashing began," a smashing, she metaphorizes, of the house of the Edwardian novel.[25] Her examples are James Joyce and Eliot. She calls Joyce a window breaker. She does not mention how *Tender Buttons* tore into the domestic space, but she might have.

Aesthetic revolutions, Woolf realizes, are not just about aesthetics. They are poked and prodded into existence by social forces and influences. Woolf might have said also on or about the 1870s, the Scramble for Africa began. On or about March of 1871, the Paris Commune. On or about 1898, U.S. businessmen overthrew the Hawaiian government and the U.S. government signed the "Treaty of Paris" with Spain and obtained control over Puerto Rico, Guam, and the Philippines. On or about 1900, ninety percent of Africa, ninety-nine percent of the Pacific, and twenty-seven percent of the Americas had been claimed as territories by either the U.S. or a European nation. On or about 1905, strikes and unrest swept Russia. On or about 1910, the Mexican Revolution. On or about 1910, mass protests by women in Britain led to new social agendas. On or about 1916, the Easter Rebellion. On or about 1919, the first of a series of Pan-African congresses, organized by W. E. B. Du Bois, was held.

In this realm, it makes a certain sense to think of the linguistic pyrotechnics of *Tender Buttons* not just as a reaction to nineteenth-century national literary conventions, not just as an immigrant's personal linguistic disorientation but also as registering, whether intended or not, the systemic crisis that was imperial globalization. The opening line of "Rooms" is "Act as if there is no use in a center." And to act as if there is no use in a center might require noticing that Europe is no longer the center because the cultures of the peripheries have remade and decentered it. To act so that there is no use in a center possibly begs the question of origin and of influence. It means venturing into the world with a shared, even if asymmetrical, concern in the disruptions of the world, one that foreshadows William Butler Yeats's 1919 line "Things fall apart; the centre cannot hold" and Eliot's 1922 line "These fragments I have shored against my ruins."[26]

It is not clear how visible colonialism would have been to someone like Stein on or about 1914. But it does seem worth thinking about acting as if there is no use in a center next to the knowledge that labor shortages led France to recruit over 800,000 *travailleurs exotiques* from the colonies before World War I. These troops and workers would be repatriated in 1919.[27] I do not want to make too much of this moment, because, of course, in all times there are immigrants, and their languages, literatures, and cultures press against national languages, literatures, and cultures. Still, the twentieth century is unusual for the large amount of mass migrations. And Paris in particular has a complicated relationship to all this. Basically, those 800,000 people who arrived in France from Asia and Africa had ties to other conceptions of the "literary." And these traditions and their aesthetic gestures became a part of the highly literate work of avant-garde modernism. These migrations not only expanded the formal conventions of literature but also broke down the conventions that kept high art and low art, different national traditions, and the oral and the literate separated. This change can be seen most clearly in the plastic arts, where artists such as Pablo Picasso directly use the forms of Oceania and Africa in their work.

So while avant-garde modernist literature is certainly a reaction to nineteenth-century national literary conventions, its resistance most likely felt crucial to its writers not because nineteenth-century national literary conventions suddenly felt merely boring or so-nineteenth-century at the beginnings of the twentieth century, but because imperialism had dramatically changed so many things. All sorts of modernists say something similar, often with a vocabulary that should make twenty-first-century readers cringe with its primitives and its savages. Still, Eliot's famous maxim "Return to the sources" is about the influence of the literature from the colonies: "As it is certain that some study of primitive man furthers our understanding of civilized man, so it is certain that primitive art and poetry help our understanding of civilized art and poetry. Primitive art and poetry can even, through the studies and experiments of the artist or poet, revivify the contemporary activities. The maxim, Return to the sources, is a good one."[28] Even in the 1930s, when Eliot's work turns from internationalism and an interest in elsewheres to nationalism, he still notices in his lectures at Harvard poetry's ties to oral traditions from afar: "Poetry begins, I dare say, with a savage beating a drum in a jungle, and it retains that essential of percussion and rhythm."[29]

Stein herself also very directly attempts to make sense of this as she does when she writes in "What Is English Literature?": "As the time went on to the end of the nineteenth century and Victoria was over and the Boer war it began to be a little different in England. The daily island life was less daily and the owning everything outside was less owning, and, this should be remembered, there were a great many writing but the writing was not so good."[30] She is in this moment saying something in her roundabout way about how those nineteenth-century national literary traditions were feeling a little less than useful in a changing world.

A *Tender Buttons* that suggests a return to the sources, rather than one that is *sui generis*, is the *Tender Buttons* that gets reprinted, after its very limited print run, in Eugene Jolas's journal *transition*. *transition*, one of the most resonant journals of early modernism, was edited mainly by the polylingual American Jolas while he lived in Paris. The journal tellingly documents the concerns of avant-garde modernism from the turn of the century to the pre–World War II period. In its eleven-year run, *transition* published work by a wide range of writers and artists from a number of different cultures. And when Jolas prints *Tender Buttons*, he doesn't just put it in the journal on its own. He insists on putting it in a larger context, in a section titled "America," which includes not only work by other American avant-gardists such as A. Lincoln Gillespie but also work from a diverse range of genres and cultures such as tales of the Aztec and Inca periods, several Mexican statues, a Colombian figure, and a Peruvian bowl.

Looking at the tales of the Aztec and Inca, the Mexican statues, the Colombian figure, the Peruvian bowl next to *Tender Buttons*, it is admittedly difficult to see them as having that same direct relationship that there is between something like Picasso's "Woman's Head" and the Fang mask that so famously influenced it. But it is not that hard to recognize that those obvious modernist forms—polyvocality, disjunction, repetition, unconventional syntax, lack of a narrative arc—are the literary equivalent of the same aesthetics that define the Aztec and Inca tales, the Mexican statues, the Colombian figure, the Peruvian bowl. That said, it is not that Stein is writing an imitative oral literature in a time of high literacy, but she might be writing something approximate to even if not directly imitative of that Aztec and Inca tale, Mexican statue, Colombian figure, and Peruvian bowl.

Still, it is worth remembering that Stein, like many modernists, is a muddled mess of politics. It is not just that she defends Weininger, but she translates Vichy leader Philippe Pétain's speeches and writes positively about him in *Wars I Have Seen*. She endorses Francisco Franco during the Spanish Civil War. A significant amount of the recent scholarly work on Stein has been focused less on Stein's earlier works and more on attempting to understand the complications around her politics after the accusations in Barbara Will's *Unlikely Collaboration: Gertrude Stein, Bernard Faÿ, and the Vichy Dilemma*.[31] But this does not mean that one can ignore the possibility that *Tender Buttons*, like much modernism, is shaped by the colonies, even if this influence is not acknowledged or would be denied. It does not let us ignore that *Tender Buttons* might possibly be a troubled and complicated engagement with how dramatically imperialism changed things. The story of cultural exchange that comes out of modernism in its less naïve moments is built more around uneven attempts at universalisms (are there any other sort?) than contained multiculturalisms or respectful diversities. I have struggled with finding the proper term for the unequal exchange that seems to define modernism that is not hybridity nor syncretism nor fusion but that also does not automatically damn with charges of appropriation and yet is not naïve in its avoidance of appropriation. There is undeniably little to no mutuality in this relationship modernism might have to the colonies yet there is some sort of creeping, undercover international migration. Maybe this is something that can best be phrased as a question: is the room of *Tender Buttons* a refuge from the complications of this street or is the room fractured and torn apart and intruded upon by the street?

It might be impossible to answer this question. It might be that the question is not Stein's to answer, that she could not answer it even as she wrote a work that seems to be breaking up and into this question all the time. By the 1930s, a diverse group of artists and writers associated with groups such as surrealism and dadaism very explicitly figure the influence of art from the colonies as a crucial one and address the politics of this influence in various ways, and in various genres. André Breton in "What Is Surrealism?"

locates the Moroccan war in 1925 as the moment in which surrealism suddenly realized the "necessity of making a public protest."[32] It is often said that European artists do not address the brutal political forces that facilitated their knowledge of, and thus influence by, art from the colonies. This is for the most part true, but there are also other sorts of moments such as the anticolonial exhibition that the surrealists organized in response to the French 1931 Exposition Coloniale. And it all gets beautifully complicated as Caribbean poet Aimé Césaire takes the moves surrealism took from the colonies and turns around and reabsorbs them to make Négritude. By midcentury, this question of the colonial will be taken up in an entirely different way by Césaire in *Discourse on Colonialism*, by Frantz Fanon in *The Wretched of the Earth*, by Albert Memmi in *The Colonizer and the Colonized*, by Stein's compatriot and defender Richard Wright in *White Man Listen!*[33] It is not that Stein and other modernists are part of the lineage of these works. They are not. These works wrestle their way to manifesto, to calls for change without modernism. And yet Fanon in *The Wretched of the Earth* writes of how "Europe is literally the creation of the Third World."[34] He is speaking of imperial wealth, of "diamonds, oil, silk and cotton, timber, and exotic produce."[35] And yet it might also make sense to think of the aesthetic revolution of someone like Stein as part of this imperial wealth that too is the creation of the colonies, of imperialism.

NOTES

1. Thomas Stearns Eliot, *The Waste Land: A Facsimile and Transcript of the Original Drafts, Including the Annotations of Ezra Pound* (Houghton Mifflin Harcourt, 1974); Ezra Pound, *The Cantos of Ezra Pound* (New Directions, 1996).

2. Gertrude Stein, *The Mother of Us All* (Music Press, 1947); *Lifting Belly* (Naiad Press, 1989).

3. Otto Weininger, *Sex & Character* (Braumüller & Co., 1903).

4. Gertrude Stein, *The Autobiography of Alice B. Toklas* (Random House, 1960), 156.

5. As quoted in Karen Leick, *Gertrude Stein and the Making of an American Celebrity* (Routledge, 2009), 57.

6. Ibid.

7. Marjorie Perloff, *Poetic License: Essays on Modernist and Postmodernist Lyric* (Northwestern, 1990), 158.

8. Lisa Ruddick, *Reading Gertrude Stein: Body, Text, Gnosis* (Cornell University Press, 1991), 191.

9. William H. Gass, *The World Within the Word: Essays* (Basic Books, 2000), 102.

10. Paul Padgette, reply by Virgil Thomson, "Tender Buttons," *New York Review of Books*, July 1, 1971, www.nybooks.com/articles/archives/1971/jul/01/tender-buttons/.

11. Alice B. Toklas, *The Alice B. Toklas Cook Book* (Anchor, 1960), 273.

12. Edith Sitwell, *Poetry and Criticism* (H. Holt and Company, 1926), 30.

13. Max Eastman, "Non-Communicative Art," *The Freeman* 4, no. 16 (May 3, 1954): 574.

14. Laura Riding, "The New Barbarism, and Gertrude Stein," *transition: An International Quarterly for Creative Experiment* 3, June (1927): 157.

15. Edmund Wilson, *Axel's Castle: A Study in the Imaginative Literature of 1870–1930* (Scribner, 1931), 243.

16. Astrid Lorange, *How Reading Is Written: A Brief Index to Gertrude Stein*, Forthcoming from Wesleyan Univ. Press, 2014.

17. Marianne DeKoven, *A Different Language: Gertrude Stein's*

Experimental Writing (Univ. of Wisconsin Press, 1983); Shari Ben-stock, *Women of the Left Bank: Paris, 1900–1940* (Univ. of Texas Press, 1986).

18. Marjorie Perloff, "Avant-Garde Community and the Individual Talent," accessed June 27, 2013, http://marjorieperloff.com/stein-duchamp-picasso/avant-garde-community-and-the-individual-talent.

19. Enrique Mallen, "The Challenge of Language: Interview with Marjorie Perloff," S/N New World Poetics, accessed June 27, 2013, http://epc.buffalo.edu/presses/SN/files/the-challenge-of-language-interview-with-marjorie-perloff-2.

20. Frances Stonor Saunders, *The Cultural Cold War: The CIA and the World of Arts and Letters* (New Press, 2013); Gertrude Stein, *Wars I Have Seen* (London: Brilliance Books, 1984), 251.

21. Raymond Williams, *Politics of Modernism* (Verso, 1989), 44.

22. Stein, *The Autobiography of Alice B. Toklas*, 74.

23. Virginia Woolf, *Mr. Bennett and Mrs. Brown* (London: Hogarth Press, 1924), 4.

24. Ibid., 5.

25. Ibid., 20.

26. William Butler Yeats, *The Collected Poems of W. B. Yeats* (Wordsworth Editions, 2000), 158; Eliot, *The Waste Land*, 88.

27. Tyler Stovall, "National Identity and Shifting Imperial Frontiers: Whiteness and the Exclusion of Colonial Labor After World War I," *Representations* 84, no. 1 (November 2003): 52–72.

28. Thomas Stearns Eliot, "War-Paint and Feathers," Athenaeum, 1919, 122.

29. Jed Esty, *A Shrinking Island: Modernism and National Culture in England* (Princeton Univ. Press, 2009); Thomas Stearns Eliot, *The Use of Poetry and the Use of Criticism: Studies in the Relation of Criticism to Poetry in England* [the Charles Eliot Norton Lectures for 1932–33] (Harvard Univ. Press, 1986), 155.

30. Gertrude Stein, *Lectures in America* (Beacon Press, 1935), 46.

31. Barbara Will, *Unlikely Collaboration: Gertrude Stein, Bernard Faÿ, and the Vichy Dilemma* (Columbia Univ. Press, 2011).

32. *What Is Surrealism? Selected Writings*, Ed. Franklin Rosemont (Pathfinder Press, 1978), 117.

33. Aimé Césaire, *Discourse on Colonialism* (Monthly Review Press, 2000); Frantz Fanon, *The Wretched of the Earth* (Grove

Press, 1965); Albert Memmi, *The Colonizer and the Colonized* (Routledge, 2013); Richard Wright, *White Man, Listen!* (Greenwood Press, 1978).
34. Fanon, *The Wretched of the Earth*, 58.
35. Ibid.